Finding Significance

5 Keys to Becoming the Leader People Are Happy to See

Marty Osborn

Here's to Success!
Marty

Finding Significance Copyright © 2024 by Marty Osborn. All Rights Reserved.

All rights reserved. No part of this book may be reproduced, stored, or transmitted by any means—whether auditory, graphic, mechanical, or electronic—without written permission of both publisher and author, except in the case of brief excerpts used in critical articles and reviews. Unauthorized reproduction of any part of this work is illegal and is punishable by law.

Because of the dynamic nature of the Internet, any web addresses or links contained in this book may have changed since publication and may no longer be valid. The views expressed in this work are solely those of the author and do not necessarily reflect the views of the publisher, and the publisher hereby disclaims any responsibility for them.

Printed in the United States of America

ISBN: 979-8-9917776-2-9

Book design by Bonfire Visuals
Edited by Jacob Ward

First Edition, 2024

Dedication

First to my wife, Lisa, whose love and unwavering support of my passion projects have fueled my creative journey. Your encouragement and support mean the world to me. I love you very much.

To my children, Jamie and Davis. You have always been the loves of our life. I am so proud to see what wonderful adults you have become and how you both have become leaders your teams and friends are happy to see.

To my business partners, Paul and Steve, for being the best business partners a person could have. For believing in me, putting up with my crazy ideas, and inspiring me to become the leader I've always wanted to be.

To Molly Hallman and Mary Selvaggio, I want to extend my deepest gratitude. For your belief in me and this project. For tirelessly championing my work, and for your expertise, guidance, and dedication to shaping this book into its best version.

I am grateful to the countless authors, thought leaders, and thinkers who have influenced my writing journey. Your words have sparked my imagination, challenged my perspective, and guided me to this moment.

To the team at Advoco and especially the operating board: Dale, Sherry, Jennifer, Michelle, Jimbo, Craig, Mary, and James. I could not be here without all of you.

To my support team: Johnny B., Alex E., Paul S., and Tom J. for taking the time to read through the book and helping me make it the best it could be.

To Jacob Ward, my writer, my "T." Thank you for helping get this book to the finish line.

Lastly, I want to thank the readers who hold this book in their hands. Your presence and willingness to embark on this journey means more to me than words can express. This book is dedicated to you.

Contents

Preface — vii
Introduction — ix

Part I
Leadership Brand

1. What Is a Leadership Brand?	3
2. Your Leadership Brand	21
3. Leadership Brand in Action	41
4. Controlling Your Ego	53

Part II
5 Keys to Becoming the Leader People Are Happy to See

5. Key 1: Stop Trying to Be the Hero	73
6. Key 2: It's Your Team—Don't Leave It to Chance	83
7. Key 3: Understand the Power of Moments	109
8. Key 4: Become a Learner	133
9. Key 5: Be Better	149

Part III
What Causes Good People to Become Bad Leaders?

10. You Might Be a Bad Leader If . . .	175
11. The 5 Pressure Points	185
12. What Got You Here Is Not Going to Get You There	203

Part IV
Can a Leader Change?

    13. An Unexpected Transformation   213

    14. How Do Leaders Change?   221

Part V
Developing Your Leadership Brand

    15. Putting in the Work   231

Conclusion

    The Legacy of Leadership   245

    Chapter 33: In Memory of Chris Oakley   247

    Sources   251

Preface
Finding the Right Title

When I first began writing this book, I titled it *You Don't Have to Be an Asshole to Be a Leader*. It was bold, a little provocative, and conveyed an important truth: Leadership doesn't have to be harsh or authoritarian to be effective. But as I shared the book with readers, something unexpected happened that made me reconsider the title.

A friend of mine wanted to give the book to his leader—someone he admired and wanted to inspire. But he hesitated. Not because the content wasn't right, but because the title implied she might be an "asshole," even though she wasn't. That hesitation made me realize the title, while attention-grabbing, was unintentionally creating a barrier for the very leaders I wanted to reach.

That's when I knew it was time to change the title.

This book isn't just about avoiding negative behaviors; it's about something much deeper—*finding significance*. Leadership is about leaving a lasting, meaningful impact on the people you lead. It's not just about what you avoid, but about what you *become*.

And as I thought about what significance truly means in leadership, I had an experience that deeply shaped my understanding. On a family trip to Florence, Italy, I had the chance to see Michelangelo's *David* up close. The statue is iconic, not just for its size or craftsmanship, but because David's expression changes depending on the angle from which you view him. From one perspective, he projects youthful confidence—from another, you can see a hint of vulnerability. In yet another view, David's face reflects deep contemplation and strategic thought.

Preface

This experience reminded me that leadership, too, is multidimensional. Just like David, leaders are seen from many angles. One moment, we project strength and confidence; the next, we feel the weight of uncertainty. Sometimes we are deep in strategic thought, and other times we are simply defying the odds stacked against us.

The many faces of David remind us that true leadership doesn't come from perfection. It comes from embracing all of our expressions—the confident, the vulnerable, and everything in between. It's about being authentic and finding significance in every facet of who we are as leaders.

That's why David is on the cover of this book. He represents the complexity of leadership and the journey to finding significance. Just like David, leaders are not one-dimensional statues; we are dynamic, evolving people, seen from different angles by those we lead. And it's in that complexity that we find our true power and connection.

Significance as leader matters because it's the difference between being remembered for what you achieved and being cherished for how you made others feel, grow, and succeed.

The leaders who are truly significant aren't just admired—they're sought out. And not because people have to follow them, but because they *want* to.

So, I changed the title to reflect this deeper message. What you see now—*Finding Significance: 5 Keys to Becoming the Leader People Are Happy to See*—captures the heart of the book. It's not just about rejecting toxic leadership traits; it's about building a leadership brand that inspires trust and creates significance for others.

This book is an invitation to find your own significance and embrace the complexity of your leadership journey—just like Michelangelo's *David*. I hope that as you read, you'll discover the keys to becoming the kind of leader people are happy to see.

Introduction

My Jerry Maguire Moment

I woke up one morning and finally had enough. I was tired of all the backstabbing, the direct orders, the lack of empathy, and the lunacy of working for people who just didn't get it. I was tired of being scolded like a child by the CEO, of being told, "You will do as I say."

This wasn't what I'd signed up for. I truly wanted to help the company I worked for, and I had plenty of ideas—good ideas—but they were shot down left and right with a phrase that left me feeling dismissed and disrespected: "Just do as you're told." I couldn't spend another day like this.

That's when I had my Jerry Maguire moment.

If you remember that Tom Cruise movie, his character writes a manifesto about the toxic sports agency industry. He's immediately fired for it, so he starts his own agency. That's what I decided to do. I was going to start my own company. A company I'd want to work for. A company where leaders treated people with respect—where people were heard, not humiliated. A place where you could try things and fail, and it was all right. A place where people worked hard but had fun doing it.

I'd read about companies like this, but over my career I'd never experienced one. I wasn't sure this kind of place actually existed, but I was going to try and build it.

So—just like Jerry Maguire—I wrote my manifesto: I was going to create a company that loved its employees and customers and put them above everything else. One that would treat people with respect and trust. Where there were leaders—not bosses.

Introduction

Then I quit my job, gathered up the few things in my office, and walked out the door.

Now, that all sounds pretty exciting. Maybe you've daydreamed about doing something similar. But I was forty-six, had a son in private school, and a daughter who'd be in college in three years. Big salary. Big mortgage. Big responsibilities. What was I thinking?

To this day, I'm not sure why my wife was okay with it. I remember asking her what she thought. She knew I was unhappy with my situation and needed a change. I'll never forget what happened when I told her about my plans. She asked two questions: "Will we have health insurance for us and the kids, and will we have some money in the bank to cover the bills?" That was it. Total unconditional love, understanding, and trust. To be honest, that's exactly what good leadership looks like!

To spoil the ending, everything worked out great. My partners and I grew our company, Advoco, to over 125 people. We were awarded the #1 Best Place to Work in South Carolina two years in a row (and humbly, the only years we applied). We were named one of Forbes Magazine's Small Giants in 2019—one of the top twenty-five small companies in the nation. We became the top-requested Industrial Engineering Co-op program at Clemson University, and most recently, we were purchased by a Fortune 100 company for an obscene amount of money that still makes me blush.

As grateful as I am for these successes, I'm more grateful for what I found on the journey to achieving them: significance.

I learned that leadership is a gift and a privilege. It's not about lording over people. It's about loving them enough to guide them into being better versions of themselves.

With the help of my business partners and countless writers and thinkers, I searched for a better way to lead. And as I strived to become the leader people were happy to see, I was surprised at how much easier it became to see myself. I dug into my strengths and weaknesses, my blind spots, and my legacy. I walked away a changed man. And I was fired up. I wanted other leaders to know there's a better path—and that a big part of what we believe about leadership is a myth.

The Leadership Myth

My partners and I had somehow pulled it off—we'd created the kind of company we'd want to work for. And it was successful.

But as the dust settled and I had time to reflect, the truth hit me hard: What we managed to do was the exception, not the rule. Most people still worked for bad leaders in soulless cultures. And most people can't just run off and build a company they'd want to work for.

That means a lot of people are stuck. Stuck working for jerks. Stuck in toxic cultures. And—this one is the most dangerous—many leaders are stuck believing the myth that *they* have to be an asshole to be a leader.

This book is my version of taking a sledgehammer to that myth.

The Power of Your Leadership Brand

The word *leadership* gets thrown around—and idealized—a lot. People strive to become leaders, but why? Is it the money, the power, the chance to tell people what to do? That was my experience, and I wanted nothing more to do with it.

Every day I see people in positions of power calling themselves leaders, but really, they're nothing more than glorified assholes. They justify their bad behavior because of their position or because they "get results." They point to all the wrong things to prove they've made it as a leader—their fancy title, the size of their house, or the extra zeros on their paycheck. But they ignore what really matters: people.

Best-selling author Simon Sinek said it best: "Leadership is not about being in charge. Leadership is about taking care of those in your charge."[1]

Your legacy as a leader will not be determined by the results you got or the piles of cash you made, but by the way you made people feel. And that feeling—the one people get when they see you or think of you—that's your *leadership brand*.

Introduction

The famous British general Bernard Montgomery said, "The final test of a leader is the feeling you have when you leave his presence.... Have you a feeling of uplift and confidence?"[2]

Your leadership brand shapes your legacy. And your legacy matters deeply—it's the only thing that outlives you.

Your Choice

Here's the good news: You can create the leadership brand you want. You can shape it into something amazing and find significance as a leader.

But here's the bad news: You might have an awful leadership brand and not even know it. That's okay—you're certainly not the only one. If you've got the stomach for it (it might not be pretty), I'll show you how to discover your current leadership brand—your *real* one, the one your team experiences. Because—good, bad, or ugly—it's there. And if you haven't been intentionally crafting your leadership brand, it's probably not in great shape.

Then, I'll help you find your *ideal* leadership brand. And I'll give you the five keys to becoming the type of leader people are happy to see, as well as some guidance on how to avoid falling back into bad leadership habits.

So, you have a choice. And it's not whether or not you'd like to have a leadership brand. You've got one. No choice there. Your choice is this: What kind of leadership brand do you want?

That choice determines everything—the trajectory of your career, your satisfaction with life and work, the impact you make on the people around you, and, ultimately, what you're remembered for.

You *can* be proud of the way you lead. You can make a lasting impact on your team. You can be the leader people are happy to see.

And it all starts with your leadership brand.

Part I

Leadership Brand

Chapter 1

What Is a Leadership Brand?

This is going to seem like a strange way to start a leadership book, but I have a confession to make: I hate the word *leadership*. Now you're immediately thinking, *What the heck is he talking about?* But what we've done to the words *leader* and *leadership* got me on this track.

When I set out to write this book it was because I was so pissed off by the way people used these words. We've mistreated them. We've misused them. And we've used them to manipulate the way we deal with people.

Think about it. When you picture what leadership *should* be, how many of your bosses or leaders have lined up with that vision?

What's sad is there's been so much written about and discussed on this very topic, but yet we see bad leaders—really bad leaders—every day.

But why?

Why do good people become bad leaders?

What's Your Definition of Leadership?

The US Naval Academy has had a long-standing history of developing leaders who have made a tremendous impact in the world. Today, a number of former Navy leaders have written very popular leadership books that provide insights into the leadership training they received.

So, I did some digging because I wanted to see what the definition of leadership is at one of the top military programs in the country. The Naval Academy leadership book defines leadership as, "The art, science or gift by which a person is enabled and privileged to direct the thoughts, plans

What Is a Leadership Brand?

and actions of others in such a manner as to obtain and command their obedience, their confidence, their respect, and their loyal cooperation."[1]

Think about this definition for a minute. Would this be your definition of leadership?

There are some good aspects to it, but is this really how we want to lead our teams? I think the part that gets me is "as to obtain and command their obedience." This is where the definition falls apart.

When you think about obedience, what's the first thing that comes to mind? For me, it's my dog. We all love our dogs, and what we want as pet owners is an obedient pet. There's nothing better than having a pet that obeys our every order. But is that what we want in our teams?

When you look at the definition of obedience, you get a lot of phrases about complying with orders, yielding to someone else, and submitting to another's will. If this is what leadership is about, then I want no part of it. Just reading it makes my blood boil.

The chilling part is when you look at the inverse of obedient: disobedient, rebellious, insubordinate, unmanageable, defiant. What does this tell us? I think it means that leaders who demand obedience view anyone who questions them as defiant and rebellious. But where would companies be without people who are willing to challenge ideas and strategies? That kind of healthy back-and-forth helps businesses find better solutions.

When I read the Naval Academy's definition of leadership, it hit me. This type of leadership had been my problem from the beginning. Throughout my career, I had boss after boss who believed in that definition. They may not have stated it that way, but they sure did act it.

For them, leadership was obtaining obedience. And that never worked for me.

Several years ago, I remember sitting in a meeting where we were discussing the launch of a new product. We were kicking ideas back and forth—what to call the product, how to market it—and the team was pretty energetic. Then it hit us.

The CEO didn't really want our ideas. What he was looking for was confirmation of the ideas he already had. To be honest, his plan wasn't great. When I challenged him on it, you could see the rage in his eyes. How dare I be contrary, rebellious, disloyal. He was the boss, and our job was not to challenge the boss, but to submit to his will.

In that moment, I'll never forget the profound feeling of sadness that came over me. I realized that for as long as I stayed at that company, I'd have to keep my opinions to myself and "respect" the chain of command. What I had to say didn't matter, and my job was to be a "yes person" to the leader.

We see this every day in companies. Leaders only want your opinion if it matches with the narrative already laid out.

But leadership is not about obtaining obedience. It's not directing the thoughts of the people who report to you. Do you want to lead robots? Or do you want to lead highly motivated people who put their hearts and souls into the business?

As author Stephen Covey says, "Leadership is communicating to people their worth and potential so clearly that they are inspired to see it in themselves."[2] When you do this, your team will soar. I've seen it. At our company, when we let the teams drive growth, there was no stopping us.

True leadership is empowering your team to be great. When leadership is working, you're not the center of attention, and your team doesn't need to be told what to do. I believe the new definition of leadership for the Naval Academy should be this: The art or gift by which a person is privileged to inspire the thoughts, plans, and actions of others in such a manner as to earn their respect, confidence, and trust to do something great.

Let's see how that can play out in the real world.

The Story of Noah

In his book *The Infinite Game*, leadership expert Simon Sinek tells a story about meeting a young man named Noah. Noah works as a barista at the

Four Seasons in Las Vegas. As Simon is getting a cup of coffee, he's impressed by Noah's fantastic service and attitude, so he strikes up a conversation with him and asks, "Do you like your job?" Without skipping a beat, Noah says, "I love my job."[3]

For Simon, "like" is a rational word—I like my job, I like the people I work with—but "love" is an emotional word. And it means there's an emotional connection.

Simon then asks Noah to explain why he loves his job. And Noah tells him that the management team at the Four Seasons really cares about him. Throughout the day, they ask him how he's doing and if there's anything they can do to help him. Not just his manager, but *any* manager. And they *really* mean it.

Noah goes on to say that he has another job at Caesar's Palace, also as a barista. But he doesn't like working there. The managers walk around making sure employees are doing everything right and trying to catch them doing things wrong. They're more concerned with the protocol than with the person. At Caesar's, Noah says he just keeps his head down and tries to stay under the radar. At the Four Seasons, he says, "I feel I can be myself."

Here's the same person doing the same job at two different places—and it's an entirely different experience. One job he loves and one job he hates. Why is this? Not because of the work or the location, but because of the leaders and the environments they've created.

Now, this story is sad, and unfortunately, not uncommon. We can easily see what's going on here, but how come the management team at Caesar's can't?

I'm sure the leaders there have never said, "Treat this employee like a number." They probably say things like "customer first" or "focus on results" or "be accountable." Company meetings are probably about the numbers and how the company is doing. They'll talk about shareholders and stakeholders, but they won't talk about the employees. And this carries over into day-to-day operations—management isn't talking *to* employees, they're just talking *at* them.

My guess is that you can tell from this story which company has better financial results.

How we treat our employees affects everything around us. It sets the tone for how we act and how the people we lead act. If we just step back, we realize we have a say in how the Noahs of the world are going to feel. We have a say in whether our team members *love* their jobs or just *like* them—or worse. If our people love their jobs, the results will follow.

As leaders, we have a choice. We can coerce and control or we can motivate and inspire.

The question is, how do you become a great leader—the kind that cultivates thriving, enthusiastic team members like Noah? To begin to answer that, we need to talk about something we all have: a leadership brand.

What's a Leadership Brand?

We're all familiar with brands and branding. At its most basic level, a brand is the way a company or product is perceived by those who experience it. It's a feeling a product or business evokes. Brands live in the minds of everyone who experiences them.

Think about your most recent purchase. Why'd you choose it? Was it because you had a past experience with that brand? Did it make you feel a certain way? Did you stay away from a certain brand because of a bad experience?

Take your phone, for example. What type of phone is it, and why did you buy it? When you think about it, you just needed something to make calls, use apps, and send texts and emails. Couldn't any phone on the market do all that? Yet you probably choose the same type of phone over and over again. Why? Because of the brand.

About fifteen years ago, I went through something that got me thinking a lot about branding. It was during my early days at Advoco, the business my partners and I built and eventually sold to a Fortune 100 company. We wanted Advoco to be the kind of company we'd want to work for—a healthy culture without toxic people. But we were having a tough time with one of the founders of Advoco. I'll spare you the details, but to put it bluntly, he was being an asshole.

The whole situation made me uneasy. Is Advoco going to be just like every other corporate shit show? Had I jumped out of the frying pan and into the fire? My partners and I decided we couldn't let that happen, and we worked out a deal that sent this guy on his way. But the point of this story is not how to get rid of a toxic partner. The point is that I woke up and realized how much it meant to me to build a healthy company. I wanted Advoco to be different. I wanted to work with people who were different. And *I* wanted to be different. I realized the change had to start with me.

During that time, I read this quote from Jeff Bezos: "Your brand is what people say about you when you leave the room."[4]

And then it hit me.

What is my brand?

More importantly, what is my leadership brand?

What do people say about me and my leadership skills when I leave the room?

This simple question changed my life.

It forced me to face myself and ask deeper questions: What type of leader do I want to be? And how do I get from where I am to where I want to go?

It changed my life because it finally brought clarity to what leadership is all about.

And it brought to life this idea of a leadership brand. Simply put, your leadership brand is what your team says about you when you're not in the room—and on a deeper level, it's the *feeling* a team member gets when they think of you.

Let's take one minute—literally—to do a simple exercise. Think of the best leader you've ever had. Now use three words to describe that person.

Think of the worst leader you've ever had. Use three words to describe them.

Those words you used—that's their leadership brand. And the emotional reaction you had when you thought of them—that's their leadership brand too.

Now, you can say you don't care about what others say about you or your leadership brand. But guess what? That's a brand.

We all have a leadership brand, whether we like it or not. We don't get to choose what other people are going to say about us, and that's an eye-opener for most leaders. Our team members are talking about us and our leadership brands every day—and there's nothing we can do to stop that. This is why it's so important for us to think about our leadership brand, address it, and become more intentional about it.

Your leadership brand will do more to affect your team's performance than any meeting, slogan, or motivational speech. Think back to that great leader you had. Do you remember exactly what they said in meetings or during motivational speeches? My guess is, you can't remember any of that, but what you do remember is how they made you feel.

That's the power of a leadership brand. It determines how you make people feel—and it dictates whether you succeed in the long run or not.

The challenge with a brand, as I discussed earlier, is that it lives in the mind. It's a feeling. And we all know how hard emotions and feelings are to change.

It's the same with your leadership brand. People will have a strong feeling one way or the other about how you are leading them. And if your leadership brand is negative, you have to put in serious work if you want your team to change the way they see you.

Think one more time about the worst leader you've ever had. What would they have to do for you to change your opinion about them? A whole hell of a lot, right? In your mind, their leadership brand is locked. And unless they've read this book, that leader probably has no idea they even have a leadership brand—yet there it is. It's real, it's powerful, and it lives in your head rent-free.

Everyone has a leadership brand. What's yours? What do you want people to say about it? How do you become the leader people are happy to see?

These are the questions we'll tackle. And let me say, no matter how bad your leadership brand is, you *can* change it. Later in the book, we'll look at leaders who made unbelievable transformations—from total assholes to powerhouses of positive leadership.

The Leadership Survey

To dig further into this concept of a leadership brand, I created a survey. I wanted to know what other people thought about leadership and what they say about their leaders when they're not in the room.

I sent it out to my network—businesspeople, friends, family, my LinkedIn community. It was a simple survey asking people about their experiences with different leaders and how they perceived the people who led them.

I received over two hundred responses, and I'd like to thank those people who responded with open and very candid answers. Here are the results.

Question 1: Have you ever worked for a total jerk?

For this first question, I wanted to use another word—asshole—but figured I'd soften it a bit. Over 90% of the people who responded said yes, they've worked for a total jerk. This wasn't surprising to me because every time I mentioned this question to someone, they'd get that little smirk on their face that said, *Yep, I sure have.* Almost everyone has worked for this person.

Question 2: What were the three things this person did wrong?

This question is where the concept of a leadership brand really took off. Now, I'm sure you can imagine the words that were used to describe these "total jerks." I'm not going to list all the words because it would take up too many pages. And just a heads-up, I left the responses unedited. So you'll notice that the answers are a mixed bag—words, phrases, nouns, adjectives—but I wanted to preserve the raw emotion in them and not clean them up. Here's a sampling of the answers:

- Dishonest
- Arrogant
- Condescending
- Self-serving
- Inappropriate
- Degrading
- Inconsistent
- Mean
- Dismissive
- Only out for themselves
- Played favorites
- Led by fear
- No sense of purpose
- Thought they were the king/queen
- Narcissist
- Yeller and a screamer
- Sarcastic
- Didn't keep their word
- Took credit for others' work

Not a very flattering list of attributes. I'm sure you could add a few of your own words to the list.

Question 3: Do you think this person could change?

The results here were a bit surprising to me: 47% believed their bad leader could change. At first glance, that percentage might be disheartening. But I see it as hopeful: Almost half of respondents believed their bad leader could get better.

Question 4: Have you ever worked for a great leader?

I was pleasantly surprised by the response to this question. Over 92% of the respondents said they have worked for a great leader. This was exciting because it meant that people know what makes a great leader and are willing to acknowledge that greatness.

Question 5: What characteristics make them great?

This question was a follow-up to question 4. Here's the list of words that came back:

- Great listener
- Cares about me
- Empowering
- Teacher
- Coach
- Trusting and open to new ideas
- Has vision
- Transparent
- Competent
- Engaging
- Compassionate
- Respectful
- Trustworthy
- Inspirational
- Mentor
- Invests in people
- Lets me do my job
- Has empathy
- Optimistic
- Servant leader
- Responsible

Now, you might think this is a trick question, but what list would you want to be on—the first one (from question 2) or this one? What list of words would you want said about you when you leave the room?

When I ask leaders this question, it's interesting to see their reactions. Of course, they don't want to be on the bad list! But this list exists. These are words said about real people in real situations. This leads me right back to the question at the beginning of this chapter: Why do good people become bad leaders? Why do people believe it's okay to be a jerk as a leader?

Question 6: If you don't think a bad leader can change, why not?

I asked this question because I wanted to dig deeper into these bad leaders and find out why over half of people believed they could not change. Here are some of the responses:

- I think anyone can change. However, the hard thing is, if they believe they have been successful the way they were, they will be reluctant to change.
- Only, perhaps, through long-term and deep therapy to get to her root psychosis and self-loathing/insecurity.
- This person was a textbook narcissist….clearly insecure about something.
- She could never accept that she needed to change anything….She would always blame "misunderstandings" on people not "knowing" her.
- Yes and no. [This person] had no direction….Went right from being a [doer to a leader]….he made no effort to make himself better.
- Probably not, they only cared about themselves and the next promotion.
- No, ego (and probably insecurity) stood in the way of self-reflection and possible change.
- No, he had been rewarded by an organization that allowed and cultivated his behavior.
- No, they think leading by fear and anger is their superpower.

Unfortunately, this list went on. What I saw in the responses was that people wanted to give the leader the chance to be better, but most ended up not feeling very confident this bad leader would change.

Question 7: Do you believe you need to be in charge to be a leader?

Only 6% of the people believed that they needed to be in charge to be a leader. It's refreshing to see that people felt this way—that leadership is not a title, but a way to influence people. I think this result might explain why so many people were so harsh in their comments about bad leadership. It seems like people feel that leadership is a gift you're given, and when you lead poorly, you're abusing that gift.

Question 8: What traits do you most appreciate in a leader?

I loved the answers to this question because they show the hope people have in leadership and the traits they want to follow:

- Empathy
- Engaged
- Listening
- Optimism
- Visionary
- Respect
- Trust
- Compassion
- Accountability
- Humility
- Openness
- Passion
- Transparency
- Encourager
- Belief in the people
- Approachable
- Thankful
- Values others' opinions

What a great list. Full of hope and positivity. A list that every leader should strive for.

Question 9: What do you think your organization wants from its leaders?

This last question is where things get really interesting. The responses to it shed light on what I see as the challenge we all face trying to become a leader people are happy to see—a leader on the good list, not the bad list.

When I asked this question, I got a mixed response. Some of the responses were about getting results and others were based on characteristics and emotions. I boiled the list down to certain words and phrases because these were repeated by multiple people. Here's a sampling of the list:

- Deliver the results
- Loyal
- Organized
- Productivity
- Driven
- Accountable
- Bottom-line results
- Numbers person
- Make money
- Yes person
- Take control
- Honesty
- Integrity
- Visible
- Understands company vision
- Make money

You'll notice there's a wide range of views represented here. For instance, some people believe an organization wants a "yes person" and others believe they want "honesty." Those are on completely opposite ends of the spectrum.

And when you compare this list with the two lists above about great leaders (from questions 5 and 8), there's not much overlap. Almost none, actually.

What does this all mean?

It means leaders are under a lot of pressure because they're trying to keep lots of people happy. And it's that pressure that makes good people become bad leaders. We'll deal with those pressure points—and how to thrive in spite of them—later in the book.

Right now, I want to prep you for what's coming up in chapter 2. You'll face some hard truths and need to dig deep to move forward.

Down the Rabbit Hole

The year I'm writing this is the twenty-fifth anniversary of the movie *The Matrix*. When I watched it again, the scene where Neo and Morpheus are talking about Neo's future hit me like a ton of bricks. It made me realize we're holding ourselves back—that we're placing limitations on ourselves that don't exist.

In that scene, the rebel leader, Morpheus, offers the main character, Neo, the choice between taking a red pill or a blue pill. The red pill will reveal unpleasant knowledge and the cruel truth about reality. It will free Neo to discover the real world—but it'll make his life harsher and more difficult.

The other option is to take the blue pill and remain in ignorance. It'd basically be a beautiful prison. Neo could live in the comfort of what appears to be reality.

As Morpheus says in the movie, "You take the blue pill, the story ends. You wake up in your bed and believe what you want to believe. You take the red pill, you stay in Wonderland and I show you how deep the rabbit hole goes."[5]

You have a choice.

Do you want to be the leader you were meant to be, or do you want to just follow the crowd?

In an interview, author and podcaster Tim Ferris said he learned this simple lesson from weightlifting champion Jerzy Gregorek:

"Easy choices, hard life.

Hard choices, easy life."[6]

Now, this is not something that's new to you. We all know this truth in our heart. Becoming the leader you were meant to be is hard. Really hard. Your mind is going to want to pull you back. It's going to question why you didn't take the blue pill—life would be so much easier. But will it?

What if I told you I could predict your future. You might say I'm crazy, but it's easy. Just look at the path you're on and it will tell you where you're headed. Andy Stanley says in his book *Principle of the Path*, "Direction determines destination."[7] So, if you're making easy choices—meaning choices that give you instant gratification or don't take a lot of effort—you're headed for a hard life. Let me give you an example.

Let's say your friend is trying to lose weight, but every morning you see them polish off a few powdered donuts. They're making easy choices—it's easy to say yes to donuts. And a lot harder to say no. Where are they headed? To weight loss and better health? Nope. They're headed for a harder life of weight gain and all the health complications that can create.

My point here is not to bash eating donuts (I'm not a monster!). I'm just illustrating that what you're choosing to do now—today—shapes your tomorrow.

Sometimes, though, it's hard for us to see that what we're doing will lead us to a bad place. With eating donuts, it's pretty obvious. But in more complex areas of life—like relationships and careers—we have a really tough time understanding why we're not making progress. Have you ever watched a friend end up in a bad situation and said to yourself, "I saw that coming"? Of course you have. And why is that? Because you see the path your friend is on, and the outcome is inevitable. Why can't your friend see it? It's a blind spot. Sometimes even when you point it out, they just can't grasp it. It's clear to you what's going on, but they just don't get it.

Sometimes—probably most of the time—it takes a big event in our life to really make us ask ourselves the hard questions and come to terms with our blind spots. When we do that and really get to the truth, that's when life gets interesting. That's when the red pill kicks in and we put ourselves on the path we were meant to be on.

So, I've got good news and bad news.

Let me start with the bad news. You can't just fix your problems. You can't take a pill or ask a question that's going to change everything. Too many people just want the quick fix. *Hey Marty, how do I get more out of my employees? Hey Marty, how can I get my team to like me?* Sorry, there are no quick fixes. If you want to get in shape, there's no quick fix. If you're having relationship problems, there's no quick fix. If you're struggling as a leader, there's no quick fix.

But the good news is, change is possible. You can shift direction and begin a new path that will lead to a new destination.

What Is a Leadership Brand?

The White Road

Last year I was introduced to an amazing company that became a client of ours—Clif Bar. I had originally heard of them in a book called *Small Giants* by Bo Burlingham of Forbes. The book is a great read, and it focuses on companies that put greatness over growth. I know this book well because one of my proudest moments was when our company was named a 2019 Forbes Small Giant. Pretty cool and one of my bucket list items.

In the book, Bo shared how the owners of Clif Bar were offered $120 million to sell their business. One owner, Gary Erickson, wanted to keep the business and live out his dream of building a great company. The other owner wanted to take the money and let the journey end. Today, the business is ten times the size, and Gary is living out his dream.

Gary's decision to keep his company despite a multimillion-dollar offer stemmed from a journey he went on many years ago. Early in the life of his business, Gary and a friend took a thousand-mile cycling trip through the Alps. During the first part of their trip, they rode their bikes on major roads and highways. Not only was this dangerous, but it was also unpleasant to be on such busy roads.

As they traveled, they'd often see smaller roads that looked much more appealing, but they never ventured on to them because none of them were marked on their map. Then somewhere in France, Gary thought of a simple solution: Buy a new, more detailed map.

He bought a Michelin map, and when he opened it up, he realized he had fifty routes to choose from, not just one or two. On a Michelin map, the roads are marked by colors. The red roads are straight and more direct, the yellow roads are moderately difficult, and the white roads are the most adventurous and challenging, but also the most beautiful and rewarding.

So, Gary and his friend set off to follow the white road. They had to carry their bikes at times, they had to ride on gravel and dirt, but the adventure and sights of the landscape set that trip apart.

From this trip came Gary's metaphor for business. He says:

"On the map, red roads are the big roads, full of noise, vehicles, and exhaust. The red road is predictable, a known entity, safe, and conservative.

"Whereas white roads tend to be smaller, less traveled paths full of beauty and great adventure. It is an unknown entity, unpredictable, and there may be danger and hardship along the way. But along with hardship or danger, there is one reward. The reward is a sense of accomplishment—the joy of the journey along the road less traveled."[8]

How do you think Gary's team acts at Clif Bar? Do you think they take the red road? Do you think when a situation comes up, they take the easy way out? Or do they challenge themselves to be different and unique?

Look at how Simon Sinek was treated at the Four Seasons. His experience was so memorable and unique that he's writing and talking about it to millions of people. And I'd bet that Caesar's is talking about it now too.

Your leadership is defined by what people say about you when you're not in the room—that's your brand. Why not make it memorable?

A team's attitude reflects their leadership. Let me say that again. A team's attitude reflects their leadership. It's our responsibility to *lead* our teams. To put them first. If you do that, your customers will be taken care of.

So, here's my question for you: Do you want to take the blue pill? If your answer's yes, then you should stop reading this book and go back to the comfort of your current reality. Go back to believing that leadership is about obedience and control and a bunch of fancy MBA words.

But if you want to take the red pill, then let's have some fun and start on the leadership journey. Let's pick our path and make this ride a good time. Buckle up. Time to take the white road.

Chapter 2

Your Leadership Brand

Arianna Huffington once said, "We may not be able to witness our own eulogy, but we're actually writing it all the time, every day."[1]

She's right. And that's such a great quote. But there are those rare moments where we get a glimpse of what our eulogy might be—and one of those happened to me.

About a year ago, I left my position at Advoco. We'd been acquired by a larger company a couple years before that, and I stayed on about as long as I could. Things had run their course, and it was time to move on.

Going into my last day, Mary, my marketing VP, asked to meet with me. I honestly had no room in my schedule—lots of loose ends to tie up. I asked if we could figure out some other time. But no, she said we had to meet today.

When we met, she thanked me for all I'd done for her and the team, and she presented me with a binder. In this binder, there were about thirty stories about me from people across the company. They talked about ways I'd helped them or impacted them in one way or another. It was incredible, to say the least.

But what I loved the most was a piece of word art that Mary had put together. She went through each story and pulled out the words that kept popping up again and again. And this is how it turned out:

Your Leadership Brand

outgoing · extraordinary · discerner · brave · reader · authentic
team · **inspiring** · respect · **friend**
inspirational · active · motivating
determined · humble · party · challenger · amiable · guide · impactful
clemson · light · heart · marty
empathetic · love · home · **servant**
brother · **passionate** · hugger · bold
galvanizer · giver · positivity · **mentor** · grateful
trust · charismatic · vision · trusted · wisdom · thoughtful
influential · **fun** · **leader** · energetic
beer · advoco · infectious · caring · fearless · advisor
enthusiastic · innovative

It might seem like I'm giving myself a big pat on the back here, but that's not why I'm sharing this. I *am* incredibly proud of it. This is my leadership brand, and I'd worked hard to try and make it something positive.

But I'm sharing this to get your wheels turning and to get you to start thinking about the kind of legacy you're leaving. I want you to think about the kind of words you want people to say about you—when you're not in the room, sure, but also when you're no longer leading the team, when you've left the company, when you've retired, and when you've gone to meet your Maker. How do you want people to feel when they think of you? What words do you want popping in their heads? How can you be the leader with a positive legacy?

The Cost of Being the Bad Boss

Close to seven out of ten Americans say getting rid of their boss would make them happier than getting paid more. That's from a study conducted by psychologist Michelle McQuaid, author of *Five Reasons to Tell Your Boss to Go F**k Themselves* (she stole the title of my next book!).[2]

McQuaid also found that 55% of people say they'd be more successful and 70% say they'd be happier if they could get along better with their boss. So, the majority of Americans want to have a better relationship with their leader. And they understand what's at stake—their future success and their overall happiness.

But McQuaid sees a bigger problem than just unhappy employees: "For organizations, it is costing $360 billion a year in lost productivity,"[3] she says. Employees who don't like their bosses take fifteen more sick days per year than other employees. They work more slowly, won't volunteer for projects, and don't want to work on anything that would force them to get more face time with their boss—and that includes brainstorming and innovation sessions.

In other words, when your team members aren't happy to see you, it's costing you—in performance and productivity. Here are a few other highlights from McQuaid's study:[4]

- 80% of workers in their 20s and 30s said they'd be happier if they got along with their boss (higher than the overall 70%).
- Only 36% of people say they're happy at their job.
- 31% feel uninspired and unappreciated by their leader.
- 15% feel completely miserable, bored, and lonely.
- Almost 60% of workers say they would do better work if they got along better with their boss.

Exercise 1: What Do You Want Your Leadership Brand to Be?

Now that you've got a sense of the serious impact your leadership brand can make—for you, your team, and your company—it's time to dig deeper with a couple quick exercises. These will help you develop your leadership brand and understand what you want and where you think you stand.

Take out a pen and paper, get your computer ready, or use the space provided below.

For the first exercise, write at the top of the page, "What do I want my leadership brand to be?" Then write down five words or phrases that you want as your leadership brand. If you're struggling to find some words, go back to chapter 1 and take a look at question 5 and question 8 for inspiration.

Go deep and truly think about what you want others to say about you when you're not in the room. I know this exercise can be hard because the voices in your head might be telling you what you think other people want to hear or what you think other people would actually say about you. We'll get to that part a little later. Right now, this is just about what *you* want for your leadership brand.

It might hurt as you walk through this because you'll reflect on who you want to be and who you really are. That's okay. You can change with some work. The hardest part of putting things in writing is it forces us to face the reality of the situation. The truth about who we are. Don't judge yourself—there will be more time for reflection later.

Go ahead and write down those five words or phrases now. This shouldn't take you long—just a couple minutes.

What Do I Want My Leadership Brand to Be?

1. _____
2. _____
3. _____
4. _____
5. _____

Exercise 2: What Would My Team Say About My Leadership Brand?

Okay, now we know what you want—or at least we have a start. We're all complicated individuals, and getting some thoughts down on paper is a first step toward sorting out your ideas.

Now take some time to think about what your team would say about your leadership brand. If you don't currently lead a team, think about what people you've mentored or trained would say. You could also think about a time you took the lead on a project or any other situation where you were leading.

You can use the space provided below or use your own paper or device. At the top write, "What would my team say about my leadership brand?" Then write down five words, phrases, or short statements that you think your team would say about your leadership.

This one's tough. It's difficult to see ourselves through other people's eyes. Just try to be real and honest—with both the good and the bad. Don't be too modest, and don't go too easy on yourself either.

Go ahead and write down those words and phrases now.

What Would My Team Say About My Leadership Brand?

1. _____
2. _____
3. _____
4. _____
5. _____

Finding Your Blind Spots

So far, you've put in some decent work digging into your leadership brand. But now it's time to take it to the next level—time to pop that red pill I talked about at the end of chapter 1.

Leonardo da Vinci once said, "The greatest deception men suffer is from their own opinions."[5] In other words, we tend to hold our opinions a little too tightly. And when they're wrong, our view of what's real is wrong. How do we push past that? One way is to understand other people's perspectives. To try and see reality through their eyes.

And when that reality is about us, that isn't easy.

This section of exploring your leadership brand is the hardest. Not because there's a lot of work to do, but because it's time to put yourself out there. It's time to get feedback from your team about yourself. You truly have to be vulnerable and that can be very scary. You have to expose yourself to your blind spots.

What is a blind spot? I think John Maxwell said it best: A blind spot is "an area in someone's life in which he continually fails to see himself or his situation realistically. This unawareness often causes great damage to the person and those around him."[6]

Blind spots can manifest in the form of a narrow perspective on events happening around you, a high sense of insecurity that causes you to be closed off to new ideas because you're afraid of appearing weak or threatened, and an out-of-control ego that makes leadership all about you and not the team.

Feedback is the key to identifying and overcoming blind spots. It's the cornerstone of how we get better. We can think we are doing a good job—a job our leaders and company want us to do—but behind the scenes, a storm is brewing that is going to derail not only our success, but also our career.

Lee Cockerell's Wake-Up Call

A few years ago, I took a writing class in Nashville with best-selling author Donald Miller. As Don and I were talking about my book, he asked if I'd ever heard of Lee Cockerell, the former head of Walt Disney World Resort. I said I hadn't, and Don told me to look into him. So I did!

Lee has an impressive resume. He spent a couple decades with Hilton and Marriott before joining Disney to work on the Disneyland Paris project. By the end of his time at Disney, he was leading a team of forty thousand people across twenty resorts, four theme parks, and multiple shopping and entertainment complexes. Lee now spends his time developing leaders across the world. He writes books, speaks, consults with organizations, and leads The Cockerell Academy.

When I got a chance to interview Lee, I found out his career didn't start so great. While Lee was a very successful manager at chains like Hilton and Marriott, it came at a great cost to his reputation and leadership brand. And Lee told me a few stories about those rocky early years as a leader.

Once, an employee smashed a bottle over Lee's head because she was so mad about the way Lee treated her. Lee now admits he was in the wrong in that situation.

But out of all the stories, one really gave Lee a wake-up call. At the time, Lee would visit hotels to check up on operations. When he got to one of his properties, he found out the manager was in the hospital. Lee asked what happened, and he was told the manager was so afraid and anxious about Lee's visit that he lost consciousness, fell over, and hit his head. That's how bad Lee's reputation had become.

This made Lee take a hard look at himself and his brand. He knew he had to do something different. If he was going to go on to become a great leader, he was going to have to change his leadership brand.

The interesting thing is, Lee was at the height of his career. At work, he said, "Everybody was telling me I was doing a great job…I was getting promoted, getting the stock options, the cars, all the stuff." Lee's leaders loved him. His organization loved him. He got the financial results and the performance results.

Deep down, though, he knew better. He knew the way he was treating people wasn't right. He thought about how disappointed his mother and grandmother would be to know how he was behaving.

So, what'd Lee do next? He got feedback from his wife. She asked him an important question: "Do you really want to be *that* guy?" Lee didn't.

Lee said, "I started going to some leadership classes and seminars. Listening. Reading more. Trying to understand more."

By all measures, Lee was crushing it as a leader. Would he fail if he changed his leadership style? He decided to press forward anyway. Being an asshole was not the right path for him.

And he was 100% right. Lee's career soared after this. Besides leading forty thousand Disney team members, he went on to create Disney Great Leader Strategies, which trained and developed seven thousand leaders at Walt Disney World. Now he talks to leaders every day about how to create magic in the lives of customers and employees.

What got Lee headed in a whole new direction was feedback. He didn't ask for the initial feedback—it literally hit him in the head in the case of the beer bottle—but it woke him up and sent him looking for answers. For all his faults at that time, at least he was willing to let other people's feedback influence him.

So, what's Lee's secret to leadership? What was his big takeaway from all the reading and learning he did during those years? He shared it with me when I interviewed him. It's so simple and so powerful, and it's become the driving theme for my life and for the book you're holding in your hands: "Become the leader people are happy to see." That's life-changing advice.

The Power of Feedback

When our company was acquired, the new company (which shall remain nameless throughout this book) offered a leadership program to former owners as part of the acquisition process. Over the years, they'd had trouble getting the prior owners to switch over to their way of doing things, so this program was meant to guide and coach owners and help smooth their transition.

I'll be honest, I wasn't interested in going through the program. When I brought up my concerns to the program director, she was open to what I had to say and offered me an alternative. She put me in touch with Trish, a business coach who used to work at the acquiring company and could offer me a new perspective. So, I gladly accepted and set up my first meeting.

Trish was a wonderful coach and ended up becoming a great friend. What Trish was so good at was getting me to look at my blind spots.

To spend time not just thinking about what I wanted, but also what my team and organization wanted.

What I came to find out was that Trish's specialty was helping leaders who were stuck in their careers get unstuck.

To do this, she would always start out by sending a 360 survey to members of the leader's team. Most of you are probably familiar with 360 surveys, even though they seem to be dying out in corporate America these days. Basically, the "360" implies that you're getting a look at your leadership from all angles.

Now, this was always a very uncomfortable task for Trish because the leader had to face their brand, and this was not something they were used to or had ever done before.

You can imagine what all those anonymous responses came back saying!

Yep, all the words we saw in the survey from chapter 1. The challenge for Trish was not getting people to respond, but getting the leader to hear what was being said without becoming defensive.

What Trish has found out over her career is that if a leader was stuck and truly wanted to continue to grow, they needed to face their brand, no matter what it was. She said it was so hard to stand in the moment while the leader read the comments. For most it's an attack on their ego and pride. We all know our brains are wired for fight or flight, and most leaders want to fight.

Trish says, "When the leader finally realizes that these comments are not attacks on them but helpful response to allow them to get better, this is when true growth happens."

Utilizing a 360 feedback loop can be so important because it can help you reset your path. It can give you ideas, thoughts, and general perspective that deep down you knew were probably true but were afraid to admit.

John Maxwell says, "You can't grow yourself if you don't know yourself."[7] You cannot become the leader you were truly meant to be if you don't understand yourself and your weaknesses. The challenge is, we're afraid to ask for feedback because we might get answers we don't want to hear. In some part of us, we know that if we don't ask, then we can act like our shortcomings don't exist.

No leader is immune to blind spots, so to deny them is like denying gravity. The misconception leaders have is that we think our team doesn't know our weaknesses. They do. Just look at the answers to the survey I sent out.

Leadership blind spots are a leader's Achilles' heel. We all have them, and they are not going away. If we don't address them, they will take us down or diminish our influence.

How do you stop that from happening? By asking your team for feedback and really listening to what they say.

Asking Your Team for Help

I'm sure just reading this heading sent a chill down your spine. You're thinking, *You're asking me to reach out to my team and ask them about what I'm doing wrong? Are you kidding?*

No, I'm not.

As we discussed, the only way to become better as leaders is to reach out to our teams and ask them how to improve. Yep, ask them.

You want in on a little secret? Asking your team how you're doing is not only for you, but for them too.

Part of a good leadership brand is being open and vulnerable. Open to hearing what we could do better and what is hurting our leadership brand, vulnerable enough to accept the feedback. Asking your team to help you evaluate yourself is important because you're telling them you care about them—that you give them permission to get real with you and help you on your leadership journey. You just have to ask.

The best part of this is it signals to them that you trust them enough to help you. That you're willing to put your most valuable asset—your identity—in their hands. Trust is at the heart of great leaders. It's at the heart of a great leadership brand.

This is going to sound a little odd, but when you ask your team for feedback, you might get a standing ovation. When was the last time one of your leaders asked you for feedback? True feedback that focused not just on what they were doing right, but also on what they were doing wrong.

We see performance reviews all the time, but the problem with these is they are always going down the hierarchy, never up. Seriously, when was the last time your leader asked you how *they* were doing? Never is my bet.

If you're determined to improve your leadership brand, sending out a survey will signal to your team that you're serious about this and that you truly want to become the best leader you can be. People talk about an open-door policy. Isn't it time you have an open-ear policy and let people tell you what they are already talking about?

It's easy to write on a sheet of paper what you'd like people to say about you. But you can't make real change by yourself or in a vacuum. You need your team to be vulnerable with you. You cannot do this alone. You need others.

Imagine if a coach never gave his team critical feedback, only praise. It wouldn't work—the team needs to know where and how they can improve. It's time to start embracing this concept and put yourself out there. Don't let fear hold you back from becoming the leader you want to be.

Exercise 3: Leadership Brand 360 Survey

Okay, here we go. The moment of truth. As I call it, the Leadership Brand 360 Survey.

Now, this is going to sound too easy, but a Leadership Brand 360 Survey is a simple two-question email that you send to your team and network asking them to help you understand what you're doing right and what you could be doing better.

The survey is simple and easy to do by design—it's meant to encourage feedback. The problem with most corporate 360 surveys is that they're run and administered by HR. They ask way too many questions that are confusing and not really to the point. And they allow HR to get in the middle of your relationship with your team.

The beauty of getting responses in your personal email is that every comment is a gift and, as such, needs to be treated as one. Think about a time you received a gift and the joy it brought you. Not so much about the exact gift, but the fact that the other person took the time to think of you. To take the time to pick something out, wrap it, and give it to you is special.

A response from your team on your request for feedback should be received the same way—as a gift from the other person. Giving direct and honest feedback is hard—really hard. Think about it from your team's perspective: You just received a request from your leader asking for your advice and guidance on what they're doing well and what they could be doing better. How does that make you feel? Scared? Skeptical? Special that they'd ask you? My guess is all those feelings wrapped together.

Your team will likely put a lot of thought into their responses. So treat their feedback as what it is—a gift. That's when something truly special can happen.

Now, we can go back and forth on what a proper survey looks like and how to create a measurement and scoring system for the results, but that's not the point. A leadership brand is a feeling. It's what people say about you when you leave the room. There's no scoring system for that—no 1–5, and no answer key to explain your results.

Right now, your leadership brand is what your team says about you. But as you begin to develop your brand, it will evolve into what you *want* your team to say about you. Your goal is to move the needle toward what you want your leadership brand to be.

The way to truly understand how to do that is not through a scoring system or a number. Who wants their brand to be a number three? No, you want your brand to be something like, "She really cares," or, "He helped me become…" But the only way to get there is to know what you're doing right and what you could be doing better. And you learn that through the Leadership Brand 360 Survey.

Over time, you'll see your brand grow. And as you continue to check in with your team, you'll see phrases like, "Stop dominating meetings" or, "Have more trust in me" turn into, "He really listens to my ideas" and, "Thank you for having confidence that I'll do my job."

Okay, so let's get to it. Here are the questions I sent to my team:

- What is one thing I should do more of as a leader?
- What is one thing I should do less of as a leader?

Yep, that simple.

Now I know you analytical people are having a hard time with this. You want details, facts, numbers, scoring. But as I mentioned, that's not what leadership brand is about. Frankly, it just gets too confusing.

For example, let's say there's a survey with a question on vision—*Does this leader provide clear vison for the job?* How are we supposed to respond? Does it mean *their* vision? The company's? The ability to execute on the vision? How do I rate them when I'm not clear on what's being asked? It's not very helpful.

Great leaders are not rated on a scoring system. Great leaders are known for how they make you feel. Numbers and results can come and go. But how a leader leads and makes you feel, that's what lasts.

Understanding what we should be doing more of, and what we should be doing less of is so important to a leader. That's why you want those simple comments directly from your team—that's what can make the biggest impact.

When I sent my leadership brand survey out to my team, I was in the process of trying to step back from being in the everyday events *of* the business to working more *on* the business. What I knew was that, as a leader, if I was in the room or in the sales meeting, people would look to me for answers. No matter how much we try to stay silent, people always look to the leader. So, I made the conscious decision to step back and let the team grow. I had confidence in what they were doing.

When I got my feedback, it was interesting to see how the team felt about this leadership move I made. Here are some of their responses.

- **Question:** What is the one thing I should I do more of as a leader?
    - "Keep doing nothing, it's working."
    - "I like it in meetings when you ask people what they think the next steps should be. This helps the team stay involved and valued."
    - "Challenge us."
    - "I like when you walk around and talk with us."

- **Question:** What is the one thing that I should be doing less of as a leader?
    - "You need to stop asking us our opinion and then go ahead and do what you planned to do anyway."
    - "Slow down. Give us time to catch up."
    - "Stop worrying about who's in the office after 5 p.m."

Let me quickly explain these responses and what was going on with my team and me at the time.

When I started writing my book, I spent a lot of time studying and reading some of the great authors and thinkers on leadership. This is something I've always done, but I took it to the next level. This had good and bad effects on my team.

On the good side, I got a lot of feedback along these lines: "Keep learning, keep teaching us, and keep up with the self-journey of being better." Pretty cool comments and fitting with my leadership brand. People were noticing the change, and they believed it was helping them and me.

On the bad side, I got a lot of feedback telling me to slow down. My brain was filling up with so many great ideas that I was like a fire hose to my team. I got so excited to share my newfound knowledge that I'd dump idea after idea on them. Just when they'd get a handle on one idea, I was on to the next.

Basically, my team was telling me I was all over the place. That I was confusing them and exhausting them as they tried to keep up. What was interesting about the comments was that they lined up with something my dad used to say to me: "Slow down, you move too fast." He'd sing it actually—that line is from a Paul Simon song called "Groovy."

And my team was right. I needed to slow down. While they liked my excitement, they didn't like the pace at which I would throw things at them. What I thought was growth appeared to them as being unorganized and unclear.

What a great response. Deep down I think I knew it, but I was sharing all these ideas because I wanted my team to think I was smart, educated, and leading by example. In reality, I was probably making them think the opposite. It took one simple question to help me reset my leadership brand.

When you keep the questions simple, you get straight, simple feedback, and that goes to the core of what we are trying to do. Leadership is intentional. It has to be. Just like playing cards or any game. The more intentional we are in our actions, the better we are going to be at it.

And that carries over to our brand. When we leave our brand up to chance, we have no say in how it develops. Leadership surveys are a critical part of intentionality. Without them, it's like playing a board game by yourself.

Most people have never asked their network or team for feedback. When I ask them why, the typical responses are, *I never thought about it* or, *I'm not sure I have the time*. But when I probe further, I get to the heart of the problem: fear.

People are afraid to put themselves out there. Who in their right mind would elicit feedback? Feedback that may not put us on the pedestal we so justly earned? (I'm kidding here.) "I'm a VP—I didn't get here by listening to other people!" (More sarcasm.)

We have been given the gift of leading people. Yes, we've earned our place at the table, but we need to take that responsibility seriously. If we want people to be happy to see us, we must be willing to hear what they think.

So, go ahead and send the Leadership Brand 360 Survey email. I'm sure your phone or laptop is close by. There's no time like the present. Once you're done, move on to the next section.

You've Been Given the Gift—Now What?

Congratulations, you've tackled the hard part. You put yourself out there and sent the survey. You just put yourself in the top 1% of all leaders—the brave leaders who want to know how to be better.

Just a heads-up—my guess is you might not get back completely honest answers. Unfortunately, asking for feedback can scare your team, but that's alright. The fact that you asked the questions was a start—a signal to your team you're moving in a different direction. People will be skeptical at first—*Why is she asking me these questions? What is he going to do with the answers?*

This is where you need to go to the next step. You need to thank the responders and tell them what you're doing and why you're doing it. Tell them you're digging in to becoming a better leader and their feedback is valuable as you head out on this journey. Tell them what you're learning about yourself and how you'll take their feedback into consideration and use it to be better.

What Do You Do with This Feedback?

As the feedback starts rolling in, the first thing you need to do is take some time to process all the responses. Is this feeling like a little too much? Does it feel like you didn't get the responses you were hoping to hear? Do some of the responses just not make sense to you? The good news is, it's supposed to feel this way. Giving your team the power to be real with you is tough. It might even feel weird. You might even say to yourself, *Why do I even listen to these people?* That question is the very reason you should. By not listening, it would be like throwing their gift in the trash. Can you imagine how that would look? How that would make the team feel? What if someone did that to you? Take the feedback and give it the care it deserves.

Remember, you did not send this survey out to strangers. You sent it to people you lead. Hopefully, people you care about, whose support and allegiance you need if you want to be a better leader.

So, take in what they said. Take time to think about their responses and the situations that might have made them respond that way. If you look at it as a learning experience and not as an attack on you personally, you'll start to remember those situations, and you'll begin to see them through your team members' eyes.

Having said that, be careful not to wallow in the negative responses. That doesn't mean you ignore them—just don't let them get to you emotionally. We had an interesting situation happen at our company after a leader took his feedback too personally.

One of our leaders, John, was incredibly upset with the feedback he got from another leader, Nathan. Basically, Nathan used the 360 survey as a chance to poke at John and say everything he didn't like about him. Luckily, Nathan wasn't in the office the day John read the feedback because John was so pissed he told me, "If Nathan was here, I'd knock him out!"

Oh boy. I was thinking, *What have I done?* This survey thing backfired and now I've got two leaders about to fistfight. But once we sat down with them and got both sides of the story, they started to understand each other. It was honestly one of the best things that could've happened.

John was an idea guy and a rule breaker. Nathan was a rule follower and cared deeply about processes. That's where they were butting heads. John would throw out a hundred ideas, and Nathan felt like he was scrambling to figure out how to get them implemented. The mistrust between the two of them was huge, and it would have continued under the surface if we didn't do the 360 survey. The survey allowed us to finally deal with it. The worst thing leadership teams can do is not be open and honest with each other. The challenge with John and Nathan was that each of them was only seeing the world from their own eyes and their own beliefs. But once they took the time to see the world through the lens of the other person, all was well.

The beauty of diverse teams is we get to look at situations and problems from many different angles. John looks at the world from a creative, big-picture perspective—*what's possible?* Nathan looks at the world from a practical perspective—*how do we get things done?* Instead of these two things being in conflict, we found both skill sets are needed, like puzzle pieces that create the perfect picture.

At our company we liked to use the term "meaningful conversations." A meaningful conversation is where both parties sit down and really dig into the hard stuff. Dig into our differences—not to focus on how different we are but to see where we can come together. So it's not just a one-way conversation, but one where both parties have a say and both parties, hopefully, come away with more knowledge and information than when they started. And that's what 360 surveys did for us—they forced us to have more meaningful conversations.

By the way, I don't want you thinking a fistfight will break out every time you send a survey. This situation was an outlier. In all the years of doing it, that was the only time anyone got so passionate. And in the end, it turned out to be great for our team.

If you're still dragging your feet on sending out the survey, my challenge to you right now is to stop and take the time to send it. Put your fear, your ego, and your pride aside and get your team on board with what you're trying to do. Their feedback is critical to your growth as a leader.

Once you've sent out your Leadership Brand 360 Survey and gotten your team's feedback, you've completed all three exercises in this chapter.

What you'll probably notice is a disconnect between what you'd like your leadership brand to be and what your team actually has to say about it. That's okay. We're going to dig deeper into bridging that gap later in the book.

Now, let's take a look at what can happen when you get serious about putting your leadership brand into action.

Chapter 3

Leadership Brand in Action

I'm going to admit something to you that's a bit embarrassing: I cry during movies. But not for the reasons you'd think. I don't cry because I'm sad, I cry because I'm joyful. When someone in the story succeeds, it makes me emotional because I'm so proud of what that person accomplished.

I'll give you an example of a movie that made me cry.

A Knight's Tale is about William Thatcher, a medieval peasant who longs for a life beyond the constraints of his social status. His one dream—which is almost unthinkable—is to become a knight. At one point in the movie, William has a flashback of when his father gave him away to a noble knight. His father hoped that by doing this he'd give his son a chance to break free from the limitations imposed by his birth. As he looks at his boy—maybe for the last time—he says, "It's all I can do for you, son. Now go, change your stars, and live a better life than I have."[1]

That idea—changing your stars—struck a nerve with me because so many of us think we're stuck. We think that we can't change who we are or who we will become. But that's not true! It has always been a vision of mine to continually change my stars and make my next day better than the day before. I didn't come from a family of entrepreneurs or risk-takers. But that was my dream: to start a great company and ultimately change my stars.

I'm sure you have a dream like that too. Most of us do. But when we face tough times, we often lose hope and start asking ourselves: *Can I really rise to these challenges? Am I really capable of accomplishing my dreams?*

You know the answer to that. Every day you get to write your story and change your stars. When we believe this, something special happens—we realize our true potential.

My Favorite Word

Back in 2016, something big happened in my leadership journey. I stumbled upon a word that changed everything for me—and helped change my stars.

The word is *intentionality*. It's not some fancy term, but it's a game changer. As I delved into its meaning, I discovered a transformative force that would guide me toward a new level of leadership consciousness, you might even say an awakening. In the world of leadership, we often get caught up in strategies, structures, and processes. But here was this unassuming word that brought clarity to what I wanted to achieve with my leadership brand and our company.

So, let me tell you how this simple word changed my life.

At the time, my two partners at Advoco and I would meet every Friday to discuss what was going on in the business and what we needed to be doing differently to continue to grow. It was one of my favorite meetings for two reasons: First, it allowed us to connect every week and make sure each of us was doing okay, and second, it gave us the chance to bring up topics we'd been thinking about.

I remember this one meeting in January of 2016. We were about to finish up when my partner Paul asked a great question: Was there a class or event that my other partner Steve and I could go to that could help us take the company to the next level?

We were doing fine, but was fine good enough? My partner Steve founded the company in 2001 as a small boutique consulting group. By 2008, when I joined Advoco, revenue was at $2 million. In 2015, revenue was $5 million. So, from 2001 to 2016 there was slow, steady growth, but it was nothing to get excited about.

For most startups that would be okay, and the owners would be happy with a lifestyle business that could sustain them for the rest of their lives. But for us, something was missing. We had bigger dreams. Bigger plans.

For me, this was my third start-up business. The previous two both ended simply when the partnerships split due to lack of success and shared vision. In each case, I just went back to corporate life to earn a paycheck to support my family, but the dream of being a successful entrepreneur and leader was always there.

So, when Paul asked us what we could do to take the company to the next level, it struck a chord with me. We kicked around several different ideas, but nothing excited us. Then I remembered this podcast I was listening to called *EntreLeadership* (entrepreneurship + leadership = EntreLeadership—I loved that combo).

The podcast was put out by a financial guru named Dave Ramsey. He'd originally created EntreLeadership as a series of courses to develop leaders in his company. The program became so popular that he formed a new division in his business. An EntreLeadership book followed, and then the podcast. What was so special about the podcast was they interviewed entrepreneurs—the everyday ones, not just the billionaires we've all heard of before. These men and women talked about the challenges of everyday business, leadership, and how to grow your company. This was us. This was me and Steve and Paul.

During one of the episodes, they ran an ad for a four-day master series class they were hosting at their headquarters in Nashville, Tennessee. So, I looked it up online and, lo and behold, it was going to be in three months. We immediately signed up for the master series, and that is when things got interesting.

Now, I'm not sure where you stand on the flow of life, but when I look back on this meeting, I see it as a sign. A sign that things were about to change. The flow of life was about to pick Steve, Paul, me, and little ol' Advoco up and change our stars forever.

EntreLeadership Master Series

Steve and I arrived in Nashville not really knowing what to expect, but we were both excited to learn something new. We'd been at it a while—fifteen years for Steve and eight for me. We were ready to see what other leaders were doing, and how this conference could help us grow Advoco.

About 150 people attended, all sitting at thin conference tables facing a coolly lit stage with a workbook and a copy of Dave Ramsey's *EntreLeadership* book in front of us. (I highly recommend this book to anyone who is in leadership and starting a business. The stories and messages are timeless, and I still reread parts of it every year.)

I must admit, I was like a kid at Disneyland when it got started. There was Dave Ramsey, who got this whole thing started. Ken Coleman, who hosted the podcast that I listened to religiously every week. Chris Hogan, the burly ex-football player with a deep voice who was a frequent guest and host on the podcast. All the Ramsey personalities were there—ready to teach me how to be a better leader and hopefully grow our company.

We went section by section through the workbook. I was writing notes like crazy and poking Steve every time I heard something we could use. Then on the second day, Chris Hogan was teaching his lesson, and he said the word. The word that would change everything: intentionality.

Bam. I'm not sure I heard the music and the angels singing in the background like the movies, but that word just hit me. I sat there and thought to myself, *That's it. That's what's been missing in my leadership. In my life. In our company.*

Intentionality is not a business plan or a goal. Intentionality is a thought process that you have every day. It is a mindset.

We were not intentional in our actions at Advoco. As Sean Covey says in his book *The 4 Disciplines of Execution*, we were caught up in "the *whirlwind* of urgent activity required to keep things running day-to-day which devoured all the time and energy…needed to execute the strategy *for* tomorrow."[2]

That was us. In the whirlwind. Not being intentional.

Don't get me wrong, we were running a good business. Our customers loved us, and our employees loved what they were doing. We were making a few bucks. But we were not reaching our full potential. We were not being the company we were meant to be. What was missing was intentionality.

When I got back from Nashville, I called a company-wide meeting to share with the team what Steve and I learned. I distinctly remember that meeting because I was so excited to get moving in a new direction. As a matter of fact, I even said, "I have become a born-again businessman!" I was fired up.

I told the team that if we are intentional in everything we do, we will double the size of Advoco in the next three years. Big words for a person who never really likes to set big goals. Not because I don't want to hit them, but more because I'm afraid of what happens if we don't. Unfortunately, I had a lot of business failures in my life. I did not want to see Advoco fail. I loved what we were doing and the people we did it with. By setting such lofty goals, what happened if we missed? What happened if we failed?

To be honest, we didn't double our business in three years. We did it in two! And within five years, we'd more than quadrupled it. We hit $22 million in 2021.

How? Intentionality. I credit everything to that word. It became our driving force.

Look, I can't give you a system to quadruple your business. I can't guarantee your success as a leader. But I can tell you this: If you're not intentional, you won't get anywhere. Intentionality has to be the underlying foundation for everything you do.

You might get a few short-term wins without it, but if you're playing for long-term success, you need to be intentional every day. And that's the point I'm trying to drive home. That's what I want you to understand before you read one more page. None of this works if you're not intentional.

But what does that really mean?

What's Intentionality?

Being intentional means making deliberate choices that reflect what is most important to you. It means your values drive your decisions, and you don't compromise your values to hit goals. It's a mindset. And it doesn't take a backseat to anything. This will increase your focus and commitment and hopefully bring more purpose and meaning to your life. As motivational speaker and author Zig Ziglar said, "Don't become a wandering generality. Be a meaningful specific."[3]

I wanted to be a meaningful specific, so that meant becoming intentional, creating a plan, and taking action.

What'd We Do Next?

When I thought about what I'd just learned at the conference in Nashville, at the core of it was an idea from Dave Ramsey: You have to give the people at your company the tools they need to grow. If your people are growing, your business will follow. And if your people—particularly the leaders—are *not* growing, your organization will either fizzle out or collapse.

So, what was our next step? How do we take what we learned and put it into practice? Yes, I was a born-again businessman, but without a plan, Steve and I would be going into battle by ourselves. We came back to the company excited and armed with new information—how do we make the most of it?

Have a summit! A retreat for the leaders of the company. Let's get the key leaders inside of our organization and go off-site for a few days. Let's get them on board with this new direction and vision for the company. And let's work through what it means to be better leaders.

The Advoco Leadership Summit

I first want to address the word *summit*. Why a summit?

When I talk about having a summit, people look at me a bit strangely. Over the years, one of the things we learned about people was that if we call something a meeting or a conference it takes on a different tone. It sounds like an event where a few people talk and the rest of the participants listen. Honestly, not very engaging.

When we use the word summit, everyone raises their hand and says, "I want to be part of that!" But if you use the other words, people will roll their eyes and think to themselves, *Not another one of these.*

What we wanted was a forum where everyone was an active participant. So, other than a predetermined flow to the topics, we let input and decisions from the team drive the discussions and results.

To kick things off and get the most out of the meeting, we had everyone read *The Advantage* by Patrick Lencioni.

I found out about Patrick at the EntreLeadership Master Series. He's an organization specialist who has amazing insights into people and businesses. He's written books like, *The Five Dysfunctions of a Team*, *Death by Meeting*, and *The Ideal Team Player*. But *The Advantage* stood out to me because it talks about why organizational health trumps everything else in business.

A healthy organization—that's what we were trying to accomplish at Advoco. We were looking for a competitive advantage, and instead of trying to look for it in a strategy, a product, a delivery method, or some slick marketing campaign, we wanted our advantage to be our people— our team. We just had to figure out how to unleash it. Patrick writes, "Instead of trying to become smarter, leaders and organizations need to shift their focus to becoming healthier, allowing them to tap into the more than sufficient intelligence and expertise they already had."[4]

The book was so important going into the meeting because it demonstrates the importance of a cohesive leadership team as the foundation of organizational health. Leaders should be aligned, trust each other, and work together effectively. And lastly, leaders should be *clear*. Clarity is crucial. Leaders need to ensure that everyone in the organization understands the company's core values, its purpose, and its strategies—and make sure everyone lives them. This is where we were failing. We had not been clear on our purpose and vision because, quite frankly, we didn't have any. Or if we did, they were created to tick a box. But they weren't relatable—to our team members or to ourselves.

The ideas in *The Advantage* set the tone for the summit and became our rallying cry. And it was a big success. We spent three days as a team working through our vision, mission, and strategy. We discussed what it means to be Advoco, and how to do justice to our company name, which means *trusted advisors* in Latin. And we talked about what it was going to take to make Advoco the company we all wanted it to be. We filled walls with sticky notes and sayings. We dug hard into how to be better and more intentional.

Going off-site and living with our leadership team was invaluable. We not only got to know each other better on a business level, but on a personal one as well. We cooked for each other, played games together, laughed, sighed, struggled, argued, challenged, agreed, and truly bonded.

The Advoco leadership summit wasn't a big success because we developed some great strategy or new vision. It was a success because we came out of it a team. A healthier team. We came out knowing our brand—who we were and who we wanted to be. And we knew that if we just lived our new vison—if we were intentional every day—we would *earn* the title of trusted advisors from our clients.

Who Does This?

You already know the end of the story. We quadrupled our growth and Advoco was acquired by a Fortune 100 company for an embarrassing amount of money.

But those are numbers. Results. What about people? How did our employees feel about working for us? How did Advoco's culture shift?

It's the middle of the story that made us successful. It's easy to get fired up about new ideas at a summit—living it out every day is hard. It's easy to cash that check from the Fortune 100 company—building a business they want is tough. But honestly, if you do it right, you should be having fun along the way. And that's what we did.

We started to think intentionally about making our company a great place to work. Making it a place people were excited about. We had some good pieces in place already. The usuals—good benefits, 100% of health care paid, flexible schedules. But we wanted to take that to the next level. What would get our team fired up?

I'd worked at a few tech software companies, and they always had some form of a President's Club—when you hit a certain sales goal, you're in the club and you get rewarded with perks like lavish trips. To me, that basically told the rest of the company, "You don't matter."

These salespeople are already the highest earners in the company. And they've earned it, but singling them out even more sends the message that some people in the company win and some don't. At Advoco, we wanted to rethink this. We're all in this together—we're truly a team. Either we all win or nobody does.

So, at our Christmas party in 2018—which was another event where we went over the top and our team loved it—we announced that if we grow 20% in the next year, we'll take the whole company to the Caribbean. We'll shut the office down. Spouses and significant others are invited too.

By August, we'd already hit the goal. So, we made good on our promise, and we did the same every year after that.

A couple years into this, a leader from marketing asked me if we could enter the Best Places to Work in South Carolina competition. I was never big on awards, but I said sure and didn't think much more about it. Then we got a notice that we were a finalist—one of the top forty companies. But it went on to say that there was an awards banquet, and our company can buy a table. And so I thought, *Okay, this is a pay-to-play type thing. No thanks.* And I kind of lost interest.

But later on I thought about how I didn't want to take the wind out of my team's sails. So closer to the night of the ceremony, I asked if anybody wanted to go. Ten people said sure. We were doing this all last-minute so they couldn't even sit next to each other. We had two people here and two over there. I made sure they knew that, but they wanted to go anyway.

The night of the ceremony, I was scheduled to be in Nashville for my daughter's birthday. So, I'm at dinner with my family, and my phone's dinging like crazy. I'm a big believer in turning your phone off when you're having dinner with people, especially my family. But I explained it was the night of the awards and asked if they cared if I checked what was going on. They, of course, didn't mind, and now they were curious too.

I'd gotten a group text from a bunch of people at the company that said, "Hey, we must be in the top 20 at least because they haven't called us yet and the first 20 have already gone."

Another ding. "Must be the top 15."

Another ding. "Must be top 10."

At this point, my family is locked in. We're all sitting at dinner waiting for the next text. Ding. "We're top 5!"

Then, some time goes by and we're not getting updates. And we get a text that deflates us: "Oh shit, I think they forgot about us." I'm thinking, *Yep, we didn't buy a table. It's pay-to-play.* It's down to two companies, and no one's thinking we could be in the top two. So, the award host is going to announce the winner. He starts reading off things this company did to win the award. And it all sounds familiar. The Caribbean trips. Our benefits. Our Chief Wine Officer. It's definitely us. Our team knows it and is jumping up, getting all excited—they're snapping pics of themselves.

Right in the middle of reading it, the guy stops and says, "Who does this?! I want to work for this company!"

That whole night was a big moment for us and for me personally. I get chills thinking about it. We'd managed to build a successful company we wanted to work for—which would've been enough in itself—and then we were recognized by the whole state for what we'd achieved. That, in turn, helped our recruiting and hiring pool and led to more success.

It All Starts with You

I'm telling you all this because it started with being intentional about our leadership brands—with my partners and I figuring out who we were, who we wanted to be, and where we wanted to go.

So, this isn't a story about how to grow your company. It's a story about how to change your stars. About how to focus on what you *can* control. About intentionally moving the needle in the right direction.

You can look at what happened at Advoco on a big, macro, organizational level and then apply it to your personal situation. What actually happened was pretty simple: We took time to reset and refocus. We figured out what was important to us. We made decisions every day based on those important things.

No matter who you are—from CEO to sales associate—it all starts with *you*. You define your values. You live intentionally. You reshape your leadership brand. And only you can change your stars.

But be careful as you begin to make changes—you've got a powerful enemy that'll try to stop you in your tracks: your ego. In the next chapter, we'll talk about how to win the battle between your ears.

Chapter 4

Controlling Your Ego

First, let me congratulate you on getting through the first three chapters. Taking time to understand your leadership brand and facing feedback from your team is not easy. As Neo found out in *The Matrix*, taking the red pill is hard and messy, but once he did, he wouldn't have had it any other way.

Getting to know your leadership brand and where you stand with the people you lead is so critical. In fact, without doing that, you cannot become the leader you were meant to be.

So hopefully you've gotten that feedback and we can keep pushing forward. In this chapter, I'm going to get a little heady and academic, but hang with me—it's for a good reason.

The Awakening

In any transformation or learning process, the first step is the awakening. The awakening is simply, as spiritual author Eckhart Tolle teaches, when you make the unconscious conscious. Becoming aware of yourself and how you make people feel is how you go from being the leader you are now to the leader you want to be.

When you explored your leadership brand and got feedback from your team, you *woke up* to a new reality. You thought deeply about who you'd like to be, and you also got to peek behind the curtain and see what other people really thought about you. Now that you have that knowledge, you have a choice. You can ignore it, or you can use it to move forward into a better version of you.

Controlling Your Ego

When you stop to think about what causes a leader to veer off course and become a bad leader, it's not because they consciously chose that path. In most cases, it's the opposite—the problem is they *aren't* conscious of what they're doing.

Remember Lee Cockerell—the Disney executive who was a total jerk in his early years as a leader? He became conscious of his bad leadership when one of his property managers ended up in the hospital. This manager fainted because he got so worked up about Lee's upcoming visit. The manager later told Lee the hard truth about exactly why he got so anxious: Lee had a terrible reputation. Lee told me: "Nobody had ever said that to me in that way. When you're like that, no one says *anything* to you."

For Lee, the unconscious became conscious. He woke up to a new reality—his team was terrified of him. Now he had a choice: He could continue being a terrifying leader, or he could find a way to change. Thankfully, Lee took the better path.

The awakening—when the unconscious becomes conscious—is an integral part of a leader's journey toward positive change. An awakening can happen seemingly out of nowhere, like in Lee's case. But the truth is, Lee was already slowly shifting how he viewed his leadership when that situation with the property manager happened. That situation sped up the process dramatically, and made everything clear for him, but the seeds of change had been planted long before. Other incidents in his career—like an employee hitting him with a bottle—could have woken him up. The reason they didn't is because Lee wasn't ready or willing to change yet.

And what got in his way? Ego. As Lee says, when you're treating people badly it's "an ego/insecurity combination." Awakenings begin when we recognize and manage our egos.

Hopefully you've had an awakening by now or are at least moving in that direction. The good news is, you don't have to wait for an awakening to suddenly occur. You can take action to bring one about, and you've likely already done that. Picking up this book is a result of your desire to understand who you are as a leader. Getting feedback from your team is another.

The awakening is just the beginning of a process that will help you find significance as a leader. It's also the beginning of a long, conscious battle with your ego.

The Battle Between the Ears

An essential part of awakening is recognizing and understanding the ego. At its most basic level, the ego is our natural, hardwired, protective instincts (fear, anger, desire, etc.) that engage automatically (unconsciously) when we perceive a threat.

It's an important part of us, and it's there to keep us safe in everyday, practical ways. But because we're humans and our brains are more developed than other animals, this protective instinct can overreact or underreact (i.e., too much fear or too little fear—too much fear can immobilize us, too little fear can get us killed). The human brain has the ability to think abstractly, to project into the future and imagine or anticipate many things, and to ponder the past in a million ways. While this is a great advantage and a wonderful gift, it can work against us.

For example, if you have an important presentation to give two weeks from now, how many ways can you imagine it going wrong? Thousands, right? That's your ego overworking. Even though it's trying to protect you from failing, it's actually working against you by creating various scenarios of failure.

It's important to note that the emotional states we experience are directly related to the stories or scenarios we are playing in our minds at any given time. Try an experiment. Think of a time when you performed poorly at something and you were embarrassed or humiliated. Keep thinking about it and picturing it for a few minutes and see what happens. You'll probably start feeling negative about yourself in a number of ways and may even begin to relive some of that experience.

It's essential to understand that, most of the time, our emotions don't know the difference between imagining something in our minds versus it actually happening in reality. The longer we focus on something, the more we identify with it.

The good news is, we humans can make the conscious choice about what we focus on, as long as we're aware that we have that choice. This is what's called a *higher brain function*. The most developed part of the human brain is the part located just behind the forehead called the *prefrontal cortex*. It's responsible for integrating and coordinating all the other parts of the brain. It's the "executive function" or "leader" part of the brain.

Each of us needs this part activated and online in order to be our true and best self. When our ego is triggered and we're flooded with powerful emotions, the leader or executive function part of our brains tends to go offline, which is a dangerous place to be mentally. And that's when the battle between the ears begins. The way we win is by getting our executive function (prefrontal cortex) back in control. That's how we recognize that our ego is kicking in to protect us and that there's a really good chance it's overreacting.

The struggle going on in our minds is a lot like the ongoing interactions and struggles in our companies. The human mind is made up of many parts, with each having its own characteristics and motives. Each part has an important role to play. For example, even the "jerk" part can actually be valuable if there's a time when a leader needs to have thick skin, or "not care" about someone's feelings too much, in order to make a tough but necessary decision.

But the jerk side of us needs to be consciously managed. Most of our "parts" or voices in our heads have roles to play in our survival. All parts need to be known, appreciated, and coordinated to function at our best. The Pixar movie *Inside Out* does an amazing job of illustrating this in a funny, creative way. If you haven't seen it, it's worth a watch. It describes some of the key players in our minds and their struggle to discover how much they need each other.

All of us have parts that are good, bad, and ugly. Usually we are okay with acknowledging our good parts (kind, generous, smart, hardworking, etc.). It's much harder to acknowledge or own our ugly parts.

But just like in the story of "The Beauty and the Beast," behind our ugly beastly parts is usually a positive motive. For example, let's say you become aware of jealous feelings toward a coworker. The healthy part of jealousy is the desire to have something good for yourself. Is there anything wrong with that? No, but it becomes ugly when our egos in their primitive simplicity want all the good for ourselves and none for the other person. That's the ego overworking again. Once we become aware of what's going on inside us, the awareness itself (our executive part) has the power to tone the ego down. It's similar to when the boss walks into a room where a bunch of employees are horsing around. What happens? They immediately shape up and chill out, right? There is great power in awareness or consciousness.

The inspiration for this book came from working with leaders who seem to have little or no awareness that their egos are dictating their actions. Or if they become aware, they justify the bad behavior.

And that's what the ego does—it reacts, it attacks, and it justifies. Most of the time, we're not even aware of the process. You think it's "you" reacting. But your ego is only a powerful set of experiences and instincts that feel like you. It's made up of your past, upbringing, culture, background, experiences, and even your ancestors' struggles and challenges.

That's why reining in your ego is so difficult. And that's why we're faced with a leadership crisis today—I'm convinced that at the heart of it is ego. But you can win the battle between your ears. Once you recognize that your ego is not the true you, your consciousness shifts. In seeing who you are *not*, the reality of who you are emerges.

A Defining Moment in My Leadership Journey

When I joined Advoco, it was my third attempt at building a successful business. After two previous attempts had failed, I still had plenty of ideas

Controlling Your Ego

and plans, though none had panned out the way I'd hoped. Despite that, something in me knew I had to try again. The alternative—continuing to work for people whose leadership styles I didn't respect—just wasn't an option.

But this time, I made a promise to myself: No matter what happened, I was going to enjoy the journey.

In the past, I'd been consumed by a desire to control the outcome. That mindset turned every day into a grind, leaving me constantly anxious about a future I couldn't predict or control. With Advoco, I decided to focus on the present and embrace the ride, whatever came my way. I realized that while success is important, perseverance is key. Each setback wasn't an ending, but an opportunity to learn and adapt.

Well, it wasn't long before life threw me a curveball that tested this newfound mindset and threatened Advoco's survival.

Advoco did almost all its business with one software company, but we'd never made our partnership formal with any kind of contract. This created a huge, unexpected conflict when the software company decided they wanted us to work exclusively with their services group. We'd always worked with their sales team, and I believed that's where we could provide the most value.

Their services group basically did what we did—they helped clients get the software up and running and helped maintain it. But the difference between us and them was that we were always willing to go the extra mile for our clients. The service group's approach was too rigid—and they wanted to rein us in because we often made them look bad. We didn't do it on purpose, though. At Advoco, we'd built our reputation on going above and beyond. Our motto was, "We solve the problems other vendors ignore." We prided ourselves on creating magic for our clients. The services team's restrictive approach clashed with that mission.

And that's why we collaborated with the sales team. They only cared about one thing: making the customer happy. We worked behind the scenes to support sales, adding our special touch to deals that needed something extra.

Everything came to a head when Advoco won a large service contract that the software company's services group had expected to win themselves. This didn't sit well with them, and soon after, the head of their global services team scheduled a meeting with the CIO of our mutual client to investigate. When the CIO explained it was the sales team's recommendation to go with us, the global services guy wasn't happy. The software company's CEO stepped in and made it clear he was going to put a stop to our involvement.

Then, the bomb dropped. The CEO held a company-wide meeting and accused us of "stealing food out of the mouths of their wives and children." He said that anyone caught speaking with us would be fired on the spot. That meeting cut off our pipeline of leads from their sales team—the very thing we relied on for business.

I'll never forget where I was when I got the news. I was in the Detroit airport, waiting for my next flight, when a friend from the software company called to fill me in on the details. I was in shock. I missed my next flight because I was so stunned. The whole future of Advoco was at risk. Was this the end of our company?

But then, I remembered the promise I made to myself when I joined Advoco: No matter what, I was going to enjoy the journey. I would surrender to the flow of life and enjoy the ride. So, I quieted my ego—which was immediately ready to react in fear and anger—and I remembered a saying I always told myself: "Every 'no' is not an ending—it just means 'next opportunity.'"

That was the moment I was truly tested as a leader. A famous quote says that champions are made when no one is watching. Well, leaders are made when everyone is watching. And right then, everyone was watching how my partners and I would lead through this crisis. In that moment, I realized that success would not be determined by avoiding obstacles but by facing them head-on.

But the obstacles had to be faced in the right way. And that was the true challenge. When you get the type of bad news I got, your mind goes into fear mode. Fear of failure, fear of looking bad, fear of letting everyone down. That kind of fear activates the ego, which jumps into action trying to defend and protect you.

The greatest test of determination in a situation like this is the ability to remain calm and focused when everything feels like it's falling apart. The best thing I could do was to stay in the present moment because the ego cannot deal with the present—it can only operate in the future. It was cool-headed determination, not panic, that would carry Advoco forward.

Fortunately, my partners and I didn't let fear or anger dictate our next steps. Instead, we came up with a plan. We launched a drip marketing campaign that included a blog called Marty's Minutes, where I shared weekly insights on leadership, life, and systems management. This helped us generate our own leads by getting people into a funnel that led to free webinars and other free content. We no longer had to rely on leads from the software company's sales team. Withing just two months, Marty's Minutes caught the attention of a large institution preparing to implement a seven-figure deal, and they called us in to bid for the work.

That defining moment didn't mark the end of our company—it propelled us toward our true potential. We showed our team that we were up for the challenge and, more importantly, we proved to ourselves that we were playing the long game—not a finite game where short-term wins mattered most, but an infinite game where our purpose and mission guided every decision.

Perseverance, determination, and controlling our egos were the key drivers behind our success. Every crisis, every "no," every obstacle was a stepping stone that tested our resolve. We learned to stay the course, adapt, and persist no matter how difficult the situation. And we didn't give in to our egos' desire to lash out. We weren't concerned with beating the CEO who'd blacklisted us. We didn't need to get revenge. We did what was best for the company's long-term success. Personal vendettas were pointless.

In leadership, especially during dark moments, you must ask yourself why you're doing what you're doing. If you can't answer with clarity and purpose, your ego will take over and you'll quit or make bad decisions. But if you have a strong leadership brand rooted in your values, you will find a way to thrive. You'll make the right decisions for the right reasons.

What I found out about myself is that for me to truly reach my potential as a leader, I had to go through this defining moment. It tested my values. And it pushed me to get beyond my ego. I was able to see a path forward because I was making decisions as a whole person—as my true self. Anger and fear were not in the driver's seat. And through perseverance and determination, I discovered that I was capable of far more than I had ever imagined.

What to Watch Out For

Controlling the ego is the first step toward long-term success as a leader. That doesn't mean that an ego-driven leader won't get ahead. We all know that, unfortunately, plenty of them do. But they'll eventually hit a wall because they're playing for short-term wins. Great leaders play the long game, and they understand that they can't do that with their egos in charge.

So, how do you know when your ego is in control? In some cases, you'll just know—and we're all familiar with those situations. You've got that fight-or-flight feeling, and you're about to blow. But in other cases, it's not so obvious. That's why it's important to pause and reflect on why you're doing what you're doing. The goal is to make decisions based on your values, not your ego.

So, I want to give you a few attitudes and behaviors to watch out for. When you're doing these things, your ego is probably in control.

Viewing People as a Means to an End

As a leader, you need people to help you get stuff done. That's a given. But one ugly part that can surface in leaders is when they see those people just as a means to an end. Like chess pieces. When that happens, you can easily let your unconscious ego dictate how you treat them. You have to see people as having worth apart from what they can do for you.

When you don't see that, you only look at the results they can offer. And this can lead to poor decision-making.

Simon Sinek says that a great leader understands that leadership is not what we want *from* our team, but what we want *for* our team.

Let's say you've got a guy who's not hitting his sales quotas. After a few months, you've had enough and you let him go. That might be a bad decision. Did you dig in and find out what's going on with him? Maybe he's an introvert, and he'd be an all-star in a different department. Maybe a loved one is terminally ill and he's having trouble focusing. Or maybe he just needs intensive training.

The ego says, "This guy's hurting *you*. Cut him loose." But when you rein in the ego, you might end up in a situation where you keep this guy around, he hits his potential, and he's forever grateful that you viewed him as a whole person—as more than just what he could produce.

Comparing Yourself to Others

In order to feel stronger and safer on a primitive level, the ego loves to look at other people and say, "I'm better than them." Why do you think reality TV is so popular? We watch *The Real Housewives* and think, *At least I'm not* that *dysfunctional!*

Our untethered egos take pleasure in seeing other people at their worst. And they enjoy seeing people fail. The sad thing is, our egos are often rooting for people to fail within our own organizations! That's truly counterproductive. If a colleague is failing, that hurts the company. And your livelihood depends on the company's success. Our wise mind or executive self knows that we're all in this together. But the ego doesn't care. It's always trying to find a way up onto a pedestal. And the best way to do that is to find someone who's doing worse than you are or whose failure might lead to your (short-term) success.

Complaining, Fault-Finding, and Creating Enemies

Complaining is another of the unconscious ego's favorite strategies for strengthening itself. Complaining implies that I'm better than them!

(Which is a way to feel better, stronger, more secure.) But complaining usually makes a situation your enemy.

For example, you're at a restaurant and they messed up your meal, so you send it back. That's a healthy way of asserting yourself. But when you start using phrases like, "How dare you…" or, "This is complete incompetence," you've made the situation your enemy. You've turned an innocent mistake into an attack on your whole personhood. That's your unmanaged ego at work.

When we criticize, it makes us feel bigger than others. And it's so easy to be a critic. It takes the negative spotlight off of us and shines it on someone else. Your ego loves this.

If you've got a compulsive habit of fault-finding and complaining about others—loved ones, employees, service workers—you've got an out-of-control ego. It's looking everywhere and anywhere for a way to build itself up.

People are always looking for the next thing to react to, to feel annoyed or disturbed by. They are addicted to being upset. We need to make others wrong to get a stronger sense of how right we are. If we can't find an enemy, we'll create one—it can be a person, a situation, a company, or a whole group of people.

Being right puts us in a position of superiority. "I'm right, you're wrong"—that's one of the ways the ego strengthens itself (but is actually self-defeating).

We see this playing out every day in politics. Unwittingly, we have forced ourselves to take sides with what we believe to be true, but is it the truth that needs to be defended or our egos? Both sides believe they are on the right side of truth, but how can there be sides? If we're really after the truth, we'd gladly adjust our views when we encounter facts that tell a different story. Instead, a lot of people dig their heels in when they're confronted with a new truth. We need the other side to be wrong so we can be right. Then we can demonize them and, therefore, strengthen the unconscious ego's power over us.

Living in the Future

Leaders are future-oriented, and that's not a bad thing in itself. It comes with the territory. You've got to hit deadlines, meet quotas, plan, predict, prepare. But there's a big difference in being pulled into the future unconsciously by fear and anxiety versus being in the now and choosing to think about and plan for the future.

Author Eckhart Tolle writes, "All negativity is caused by an accumulation of psychological time and denial of the present. Unease, anxiety, tension, stress, worry—all forms of fear—are caused by too much future, and not enough presence. If you want peace, live in the now..."[1]

When you're always attempting to live in the future, you're anxious. And when you're anxious and afraid, your ego is on high alert. It's scanning the horizon, seeing who it can use or abuse to make itself feel safer. You won't consciously know this is happening—you might not even know you're feeling fear. Be aware of this. Don't let your ego take the lead.

The Voices Inside Your Head

All people hear voices in their heads. Some people say, "I'm just having thoughts." Okay, well that's probably true. But if we pay attention to our many thoughts, we'll quickly begin to see that the thoughts vary a great deal in terms of tone, intensity, and motive.

For the sake of this discussion, let's just call them voices. Most of the voices we hear are facets of our instinctive protective egos on overdrive. One voice will say, "Say that to him!" And another will say, "Don't do that, it will just turn into an argument!" A third voice might chime in, "Oh, forget the whole thing, it's pointless!" And then other voices might chime in on this or about a thousand others subjects that the ego thinks are important for surviving the day.

Sometimes the voices go to the dark side and say things like, "This person hates you." Or, "It's hopeless." Almost always the voice of the untethered ego is pulling us into the past or the future: "I'm angry at Fred for embarrassing me last week," or, "I'm afraid I'm not going to hit my goal for sales this month."

The discomfort or pain of all this noise is why many people turn to things like drugs, alcohol, addictive shopping, overeating, smoking, excessive TV, scrolling the Internet, workaholism, etc. These things quiet the voices by dulling or distracting the mind and pulling our consciousness below all the noise.

Now occasionally, we may hear a voice that is different. This voice is calm and kind, reassuring and confident, unhurried, and quietly but firmly guiding us to be or do something. This is the voice of the wise mind, or executive function, or higher self, or leader self, or the conscious self. The actual name varies depending on which philosophical or spiritual perspective you might have. Call it what you want, but this is the part of us humans whose job it is to manage and coordinate all the urgent voices that are conflicted and trying to get us to do the impossible (change the past, control the future).

Our essential task as leaders—and as people—is to quiet the voices in healthy ways so the executive part of us can come online and do its job of sorting through the many thoughts and extracting the kernels of truth each one is trying to express. This will enable us to function at our best and operate as our *true self*. And that's the goal. The true self emerges when you're led by your conscious values, not by your ego. In contrast, the false self is your ego-driven self—the self that just reacts without thinking.

I bring all this up because as we start to look at the five keys to becoming the leader people are happy to see, you need to be aware of the voices in your head and understand that though they are trying to protect you, they can quickly misguide you if you take them too seriously. My guess is they're talking to you now as you read this section. And they were probably talking to you when you were building out your leadership brand and getting feedback from your team.

The ego voices want to make you feel correct. As you make your leadership brand conscious, it can become difficult because the ego wants you to be right, but part of growing as a leader involves admitting when you're wrong. When you find yourself comparing, criticizing, creating

Controlling Your Ego

enemies, or living too much in the future, take a step back and quiet the voices (how to do this will be discussed later in this chapter). You'll probably feel a stronger impulse to do those things when you're under a lot of pressure. That's a pretty common place to be as a leader. And it's often when the false self tries to take the reins.

The better you understand the inner workings of your mind, the easier it will be to manage your impulses and let your true self take control.

Let's take a look at what happens to a leader when they mismanage their impulses and let their ego take the lead.

Take One for the Team

My sister was a first grade schoolteacher in the New York State public school system. She's retired now, but she told me a story recently about an issue she had with the school's principal.

The problem started at the beginning of the school year. That's when the school sends student assessments to the district. They do this to see how the students measure up to the standards. Well, the principal didn't like where the kids were at. So, she massaged the results a bit and made it seem like the students were doing better than they really were. That was her ego at work—she acted out of a fear of what district leaders would think of her.

Later in the year, the kids took another test to see where they were at. But this one couldn't be massaged. The principal didn't quite think that through when she adjusted the results in the beginning of the year. So now there's a problem. The kids scored lower on this test—so it looks like they got worse over the course of the school year, which means it looks like my sister's teaching caused a decline in their scores. The truth was that their scores went up—but not according to the numbers the district had.

When the principal found out about this, she owned up to it and took the heat. Just kidding. She tried to dodge the bullet. She sat down with my sister and asked her to "take one for the team." She wanted my sister to say it was her fault. Once again, that's the ego at work. What's really interesting—and upsetting—is that the principal was willing to just keep digging a deeper hole. She was ready to lie, sacrifice other people's careers, and pull others into an unethical scheme. This was a woman who let her ego take the lead. And it's a clear example of how destructive that can be.

Talk about making my blood boil. A true leader never says, "Take one for the team." A true leader always accepts responsibility for their actions in addition to the actions of their team. "Taking one for the team" is the responsibility of the leader. How can a leader manage their team when they abdicate responsibility? How can a team respect their leader if they know when the going gets tough, their leader will not be there for them?

There's a great lesson here: It's so important to understand how the actions you take will affect everyone involved. The principal was trying to get a short-term win, but she did long-term damage in the process. By focusing on propping up her false self—the self who can't lose, the self who doesn't make a mistake—she hurt her reputation, integrity, and team's morale. Probably for a long time to come.

Moving from the False Self to the True Self

It's easy for us to think we'd never want to act like that principal. Her mistakes are so obvious, and her poor leadership is on full display. But I doubt the principal woke up one day and decided to become a bad leader. Instead, she made a series of bad decisions that served her false self. If she'd committed to developing her true self, she would have behaved in a way that served her values, not her fears.

Developing your true self allows you to take ownership of your mistakes because there's no reason to pretend you're perfect. It keeps you from acting out of fear and anxiety. And it helps you pause and consider the long-term effects of your actions.

As you continue to develop your leadership brand, make sure your true self is driving the process. Don't let your ego take control. Don't become the type of leader others want you to be. Become the leader you know you

Controlling Your Ego

need to be. Quiet the ego and understand what you truly value and who you truly are.

This shift—from your ego-driven false self to your values-driven true self—is actually pretty simple. Let me be clear, though: It's not easy. Not at first, anyway. You have to consciously be aware of yourself and how you're behaving every day, in every moment. But it does become easier and more reflexive over time. Here's the simple process you can use in everyday situations to move toward your true self:

Step 1: Recognize what your ego instincts are and when they are starting to take over. The obvious signs that the ego is being triggered are when we feel offended, upset, angry, defensive, afraid, hurt, unheard, belittled, or when we want to control or get revenge. Even mild feelings of irritability or discomfort are indicators that our protective ego instincts are being triggered.

Step 2: You need to quiet the agitated voices of your mind so the leader or wise part of you can come back online and assess the situation. In other words, calm yourself down so you can hear what your various upset parts are trying to communicate. There are lots of ways to do this, and I've included some exercises and methods in the next section.

Step 3: Once you've quieted the ego, you can then take action to address the situation in an integrated way that is safe and effective.

Let's see how using this process would have helped the principal at my sister's school. I'm going to walk through the principal's situation and show how things could have played out differently if she'd applied this simple three-step process.

- **Step 1:** The principal sees the students' poor test scores, gets anxious, and has an idea: She could adjust the results to make them better. But instead of moving forward with the idea and considering how she could pull it off, she recognizes that fear is driving her thoughts. She's aware that her ego is trying to protect her because bad student scores reflect poorly on her.

- **Step 2:** She stops and takes a deep breath. She acknowledges her fear but doesn't let it control her. She wonders, *Why am I so afraid right now?* After exploring that question, she considers her values. Would being deceptive reflect who she wants to be as a leader? It wouldn't, so she abandons the idea of changing student scores.
- **Step 3:** She brainstorms ways to help students excel this school year. Over the next few weeks, she meets with senior teachers and comes up with a plan that reflects her and the school's values.

Following that process could have saved the principal's reputation and leadership brand. But let me point out that it would have only saved her that day and in that moment. Using this process is not a one-and-done thing. It has to be used repeatedly every day to help you step into your true self. Working this process into our lives is a skill, and like any skill, it becomes easier over time.

Now, the ego-driven false self might rear its head from time to time. You can't beat yourself up when that happens. Own up to your mistake and make it right. Your ego might fight you on that, but it's a necessary step so you can continue becoming the best version of yourself.

Ways to Quiet the Noise of the Ego

There are lots of ways to slow down and quiet the noise of the ego: meditation, yoga, prayer, mindfulness practices. We won't go in depth on all these, but here are a few tips that can help you get started:

- **Learn and practice a simple form of meditation.** This should be something that makes sense to you, is easy to do, and that you can do almost any place and any time. The core elements of meditation are a repeating focus (word or phrase, image that you picture, etc.) and practicing letting go of interfering thoughts and distractions (I hear the people in the next room, but I'm just going to let that go and return to my focus).
- **Use your five senses to focus on the present moment.** This will take your focus away from relentless thoughts. A good starting

place is focusing on the sensations of your breath, the sounds that are happening around you, or what you can see. Doing this brings us back into the now and in touch with our bodies and environment.

- **Use encouraging sayings or affirmations to focus and comfort yourself and bring you into the present moment.** Here are some examples: "I have nowhere else to be except here and now...so I'll work with it." "I surrender to the now." "Do the next right thing in the present moment."

These methods can help you control your ego and react better to stressful situations. They're particularly helpful to use in step 2 of the three-step process we've been discussing. They'll allow you to pause in the moment and quiet the ego.

I'd also recommend practicing things like meditation and prayer every day. It can help you become more reflective about how you've acted in the past and how you'd prefer to act in the future. This will solidify your values and move you toward becoming your true self.

Okay, I know that was a lot, and I'm grateful you stuck with me. The ego and becoming conscious aren't easy topics, but they're so important to understand as you become a better leader.

In the next part of the book, we'll take a more practical path and discuss the five keys to becoming the leader people are happy to see.

- Key 1: Stop Trying to Be the Hero
- Key 2: It's Your Team—Don't Leave It to Chance
- Key 3: Understand the Power of Moments
- Key 4: Become a Learner
- Key 5: Be Better

These keys will help you unlock your potential and your team's, build your leadership brand and your legacy, and become the leader you were meant to be.

Part II

5 Keys to Becoming the Leader People Are Happy to See

Chapter 5

Key 1: Stop Trying to Be the Hero

I had just finished up a company leadership summit and was on the airplane about to take off for home. It was an amazing week with my team working though how our company was doing, what we could be doing better, and prioritizing what we were going to be doing next.

Then we got the dreaded message. "Ladies and gentlemen, I am sorry to report we have a problem with the right engine, and we have called maintenance to come out and look at it."

Yikes, I wonder how long this is going to take. So, with some time to kill I decided to pull out a book my marketing leader gave me called *StoryBrand* by Donald Miller.

Now, I'm not sure if you have read *StoryBrand* or not, but if you haven't, it is a must-read for any business leader.

When I first started reading, I assumed it was a marketing book and my team wanted me to read it so I would understand a little more about what they wanted to do with our website. But boy, was I wrong. This book hit me right at the beginning. This was more than a marketing book—it was a leadership book, and it was telling me our approach to consulting was wrong. I got so excited that while I was sitting on the plane, I called our business coach, Chris, and said we have to have the team read this book now.

There was just one problem: The day before, we'd all selected the next book we would read as a group. We did that at the end of every summit

Key 1: Stop Trying to Be the Hero

meeting. That way, we could read it before the next summit, where we'd discuss it together.

Chris's reaction to my call was the best. He knows I can get excited about new things, but he was like, "Marty, we haven't even left the retreat and you already want to change the plan we all agreed on?" I said, "Yes, we need to change it now. You need to read this book, and I think you'll agree this may be one of the most important lessons we learn as leaders."

Well, now I had Chris's attention. What could be in this book that is so exciting that we must change everything we're doing? So, I started to explain.

What Donald Miller talks about in the book is that in every great story, there's a hero on a journey trying to overcome challenges and achieve their goals. Sounds a lot like running a business. But what Miller argues is that, as a business, you shouldn't position yourself as the hero. Instead, you should embrace the role of the *guide* who empowers your customers to become the heroes of their own stories. Let me repeat that. We should embrace the role of the guide who empowers our customer to be the hero of their own story.

Let's think about this in terms of the movie *Star Wars*. Who's the hero? Luke Skywalker. And who's the guide? Our little green friend Yoda. He helps Luke on his quest to become an awesome Jedi and defeat the Galactic Empire. So, your company needs to play the role of Yoda. You're not the hero or the main character—the customer is.

This goes against everything that we've been taught. This even goes against Maslow's hierarchy of needs, where at the top of the pyramid is self-actualization. But I think Maslow got it wrong. We were getting it wrong at Advoco too.

When you think about what causes bad customer service, it's because we think we are the hero of the story. Nothing turns off another person more than this concept. We've all met the salesperson who makes their company the hero. They talk about how great their company is—the revenue, the growth, how long they've been in business—until your eyes gloss over. Or you've visited websites like that—the company sings its own praises and tells a long origin story, but all you're wondering is, *How can you help me solve my problem?*

We need to be our customers' guide, not the hero. We need to listen to them and figure out what winning looks like for them. We need to help them slay their dragons, conquer their obstacles, and crush their goals.

One of the concepts of business and leadership I learned early on—and it has stuck with me my whole career—is a quote from Zig Ziglar: "You will get all you want in life, if you help enough other people get what they want."[1] Boom—be the guide.

And then it hit me: This idea can go beyond just the business/customer relationship. It applies perfectly to leadership. When leaders position themselves as the heroes, they spend so much time focusing on their own goals and agendas, they have no idea how to help their teams.

But isn't that the point of leadership—to help our team members win and become the best versions of themselves that they can be?

We see this play out in story after story. It's called the "hero's journey," and you can see it unfold in just about any movie or TV show. The hero embarks on a journey filled with obstacles. Then he seeks guidance from a wise mentor or guide. That guide helps the hero defeat their enemies and complete their quest.

Your team is the hero. And they're looking for a guide who can help them navigate the challenges they face. By positioning yourself as the guide, you play a crucial role in their narrative.

Lessons from a Sitcom

I think one of the best examples of being a guide comes from the Apple TV sitcom *Ted Lasso*.

In the show, the lead character is an American football coach who is hired to coach a struggling English soccer team, despite having no experience in the sport. Throughout the series, Ted Lasso acts as a mentor

Key 1: Stop Trying to Be the Hero

and guide to the players, the team staff, and even the club's owner, Rebecca.

When you talk to most people, their first reaction to the show is that Ted is the hero and he has come to save the day for this struggling football club. But as the story unfolds, we see Ted in a different light.

Ted Lasso's main focus is on supporting and empowering the team members. He recognizes their individual strengths and weaknesses and works toward building a cohesive unit. Rather than using harsh criticism or a domineering leadership style, he adopts an approach rooted in empathy, positivity, and genuine care for his players' well-being.

As an American coach in England, he faces cultural differences that could potentially hinder his ability to connect with the team. But he approaches these differences with curiosity, open-mindedness, and respect. And that earns him the respect of the team.

He also leads by example. His team sees him act with integrity, humility, and kindness. If he says he'll do something, he'll do it. His team quickly learns they can trust him.

Beyond his role as a coach, Ted serves as a guide for his colleagues' personal lives as well. He listens, offers advice, and helps them navigate challenges outside the soccer field. His genuine interest in the well-being of those around him extends beyond the game, making him a trusted guide in their personal journeys.

Lastly, Ted's optimistic, and he genuinely believes in his team. Eventually, this rubs off on the players, and they start to believe in themselves. Ted has created a culture where they feel valued and supported, which makes them more confident. After a while, the unthinkable happens—they start to win!

I know this is just a sitcom, but it's a great example of a leader being the guide and not the hero. Just like any great story, it's got lessons that can be applied to real life.

I think the show gets summed up best in the last episode. (Spoiler ahead if you haven't watched the show!) A sports journalist finishes writing a book about Ted's leadership. When he asks Ted to review the book, which the journalist named *The Lasso Way*, Ted gives him the draft back with a simple note: "One small suggestion, I'd change the title. It's not about me. It never was."[2]

That was it. He was never the hero of the story. His team and organization were. Ted was just the guide.

Ted didn't look at coaching as a way to promote himself. Instead, he saw it as an opportunity to positively impact the lives of his players. His ultimate focus was on helping people grow, building relationships, and creating a positive culture within the team.

How would you describe Ted Lasso's leadership brand? Would he be a leader you'd be happy to see?

I think we'd all say yes to that question. And that's because great leadership is about being the guide, not the hero.

What Is a Guide?

Let's dig a little deeper into what a guide is. I think it will help us as we walk through how you can move from being the hero to being the guide.

In the context of business and leadership, a "guide" typically refers to someone who provides direction, support, and advice to help individuals or organizations achieve their goals or navigate challenges. A guide can be a mentor or coach who shares their expertise and experience with others. They offer guidance on professional development, decision-making, and career advancement.

When we look for great examples of guides outside of the movies or TV, the first people that come to mind for me are the Sherpas.

The term "Sherpa" refers to an ethnic group native to the Himalayan region, primarily in Nepal, although there are also Sherpa communities in other parts of the Himalayas. Sherpas are well-known for their expertise in mountaineering and their crucial role in supporting climbers and expeditions in the high-altitude and challenging terrain of the Himalayan mountains, including Mount Everest.

Key 1: Stop Trying to Be the Hero

Sherpas are renowned for their ability to navigate treacherous mountain terrain, set up climbing routes, and manage logistics for expeditions. They have a deep understanding of the Himalayan environment. Sherpas are hired as guides, porters, and support staff for climbers attempting to summit peaks in the Himalayas. They are known for their strength and endurance at high altitudes, which is crucial for assisting climbers in reaching their goals.

What is amazing about this group of people is the reputation (brand) they have achieved leading and guiding people. They're known all over the world—by climbers and people who've never set foot on a mountain. If someone calls you a Sherpa outside the context of mountaineering or the Himalayan region, it's used metaphorically to describe your role as a guide, mentor, or expert who helps others achieve their goals. It means you know what it takes to cross the finish line.

If the Sherpas have achieved such high regard, what lessons can we learn from them about being the guide and leading people to incredible feats?

As I studied the Sherpas and their difficult role of leading people on very dangerous expeditions to the top of Everest, four critical lessons became apparent:

1. **They must guide the whole team to the top.** Success is not having one person make it, but the whole team. As a leader, a Sherpa has to make sure they help everyone reach their potential. Getting to the top is not about them, but the people who entrusted their lives to them. How successful would they be if they said, "Well, I made it to the top and only lost half the team"? Here's the takeaway: The more we make it about others, the more success we will enjoy.

2. **They understand detailed planning saves lives.** Intentionality. We talked about this at length in chapter 3, but we see this concept come up again and again. If you know anything about scaling the most dangerous mountain in the world, planning is paramount.

You cannot get to the top if you don't have a plan. Great leaders intentionally plot out each step of an undertaking. They understand where their team is headed.

3. **They expect and plan for setbacks.** Sherpas routinely deal with bad weather and unexpected obstacles. But they're not derailed by them. They build contingency plans and adapt. Just like business and life, nothing will ever go as exactly as we want it to. We will always have setbacks and some sort of conflict. To be successful you need to learn to enjoy the challenges while you are solving them. There is beauty and learning in everything we experience. We just need to adjust our perception.

4. **They walk with their teams.** I think this is one of the most important and powerful characteristics. Sherpas climb the mountain with you. As a result, they build trust and increase the odds of success. You can't ask your team to do something you aren't willing to do. We see so many leaders who are disconnected from their teams. Either they feel like they are too important to spend time with them or they just overcommit their time trying to be the hero, which leaves them with no time to be the guide. Could you imagine hiring a guide to help you get to the summit and instead of leading you, they handed you a map and stayed at base camp? How would that make you feel? A leader who doesn't walk alongside their team might think they're leading by example. Or they might think the team gets it—they're an important, busy leader. But what they're really communicating is that the team isn't a priority.

Today's business climate is changing so rapidly. What we need are Sherpa-like leaders who are bold, courageous, thoughtful, and adaptable.

How About a New Type of Leadership?

I think we need a new kind of leadership. But before I explain what I mean, I think it's important to define our traditional ideas about what a

Key 1: Stop Trying to Be the Hero

guide is and what a leader is. They overlap in some areas, but they also have distinct characteristics. Here's what I see:

Guide:

1. **Provides navigation:** A guide primarily assists and directs people as they navigate specific situations or challenges. Their role is often to provide information, advice, and support to help others make informed decisions and reach particular objectives.

2. **Offers expertise and knowledge:** Guides typically possess expertise or specialized knowledge in a particular field or skill set. They rely on their knowledge and experience to provide valuable guidance and insights to those they are assisting.

3. **Fills a temporary role:** Guides often serve in a temporary or specific capacity. For example, a tour guide may lead a group through a city for a few hours, and a wilderness guide may help hikers complete a specific trail. Their guidance is usually situation specific.

4. **Operates as a peer:** The relationship between a guide and the individuals they are guiding is generally less hierarchical. Guides aim to empower others by providing information and support, but they may not necessarily make decisions on behalf of those they are guiding.

5. **Focuses on goals:** Guides typically help others achieve specific goals or complete tasks efficiently. Their guidance is often focused on achieving a particular outcome.

Leader:

1. **Provides direction and vision:** A leader provides direction, vision, and purpose to a group or organization. They set goals, define a strategic path, and inspire others to follow them toward a common objective.

2. **Offers influence and inspiration:** Leadership is often associated with the ability to influence and inspire others. Leaders motivate and guide their team or followers by setting an example, setting expectations, and creating a sense of purpose and unity.

3. **Fills a long-term role:** Leadership roles are often ongoing and involve sustained responsibility for a group, team, or organization. Leaders are responsible for decision-making, problem-solving, and overall direction over an extended period.

4. **Operates in a hierarchy:** I don't endorse hierarchical thinking, meaning you shouldn't need to leverage your title or position to be an effective leader. But leadership roles are typically part of a hierarchical structure with leaders at the top. They have authority and decision-making power within their domain.

5. **Focuses on broader objectives:** Leaders are concerned with the broader success and well-being of their group or organization. Their focus extends beyond specific tasks or situations to include overall strategy, culture, and sustainability.

I'd like to see these two lists merge into something I call *guidant leadership*. When we look at the leader list, we can all nod our heads in agreement with each point. With the guide list, maybe it's not so clear how a leader should adopt all those behaviors—particularly when it comes to filling a temporary role and operating as a peer. But I think leaders need to act as guides far more often than they do.

We need to come alongside our team members and help them on the ground, right where they're at. We need to be experts in their areas of knowledge so we can help them achieve their goals and offer meaningful advice. We need to work alongside them as peers to build morale and help them navigate problems—not by telling them exactly what to do, but by empowering them to make good decisions.

And finally, we need to know when to do these things. What I mean is, we cannot be walking alongside our team members at all times—but we should have our finger on the pulse of our team so we know when we should put on that guide hat and jump in the trenches with them. And we should have a sense of what each team member needs from us at any specific moment.

That's what I mean by guidant leadership. It's a hands-on approach to leadership that finds a balance between managing the big-picture objectives and helping our team members as individuals.

So much has been said and written about servant leadership, but I think guidant leadership is a more helpful and powerful concept. To me, servant leadership has a nice sound to it, but it really misses the mark in a practical sense. To be a servant means to be one that serves others—one that performs duties for a person. I'm not thinking that is what we want in our leaders. Yes, leaders need to be of service sometimes, but a great leader does so much more. Think about the words people used in chapter 1 when I asked them to describe a great leader they'd worked for: teacher, coach, mentor, visionary, empowering, inspirational. That's way beyond serving and requires an entirely different set of skills and abilities.

That's a guidant leader. Someone who sees a path to the future, boldly steps out onto it, inspires others to join them, and empowers them along the way.

Stop being the hero leader and become the guidant leader. You'll never regret making that investment in your team.

Chapter 6

Key 2: It's Your Team—Don't Leave It to Chance

I have to admit something: I was terrible at hiring people. Yep, it was not my strong suit.

If you asked my team to name one of my biggest weaknesses as a leader when we were growing the company, they'd say I was bad at hiring. The good news is, I got better.

And my path to improving started at the Ramsey EntreLeadership conference I talked about in chapter 3. I was there sitting in a session about hiring, firing, and personal testing when I realized I'd never spent any time studying or even thinking much about these topics. To be honest, I felt like hiring was a necessary evil of building a team. I didn't enjoy it, and I definitely didn't approach it with intentionality.

But then I heard the stories of how Ramsey Solutions did its hiring, and I was stunned.

The first thing they said was *slow down*. The biggest cause of making bad team member choices is hiring too fast. Leaders have trouble with this because during the hiring process, they're thinking, *I don't have time for this!* But when you hire fast, you tend to use your gut, not your brain. And that leads to bad hires.

Key 2: It's Your Team—Don't Leave It to Chance

At Ramsey, they have a minimum of six interviews and often go as high as fifteen. And before anyone is hired, they do a spousal dinner, which means the leader and their spouse have dinner with the candidate and their spouse (if they have one). They do this for two reasons. First, meeting the candidate's spouse gives you insight into their marriage dynamic. Whatever's going on at home will eventually make its way into work. And while you obviously can't get a perfect read on their relationship, you can at least rule out extreme situations. Second, the leader's spouse gets a chance to meet the candidate. And if anyone can sniff out a problem, it's our spouses.

Wow. Up to fifteen interviews. Spousal dinner. The whole process takes three months! Oh, and by the way, every candidate has to take the DISC profile test to let the interviewer know how you like to operate and consume information. (We'll talk more about the DISC later.)

If I asked you what the most important skill a leader needs to have is, what would you say? When I ask this question, I get answers that are all over the place. Sales, marketing, finance, etc. All great things, but here's what I've found: To be a great leader, you need to be great at hiring.

Now, I'm not saying you have to be the person doing all the work, but the leader needs to set the process, the pace, and the criteria for making a decision.

So many leaders leave this up to chance. And I know that's true because when I ask them how many interviews they do to vet a new hire, it's nowhere near fifteen and rarely near six. In fact, six or more interviews scares them. If that number scares you too, then I have bad news: You're not good at hiring. Trust me, you're not. But the good news is, *you can be* because hiring is not an art form, it's a skill. A skill that can be learned. A skill that can be honed, and a skill that you will get better at over time.

Hiring is lot like fishing. I'm not sure if you've ever gone fishing, but anyone who has knows that if you don't have the right tools or the right locations, no matter what you do, you are not going to catch any fish. The people who catch fish have either taken the time to learn the skill of fishing—with the right bait, the right fishing tackle, the right times and locations—or they hired a guide.

In this chapter, I want to walk you through the process we used to hire over one hundred engineers. At Advoco we had less than 1% turnover, and we were able to hire as many people as we needed when everyone around us was saying that there were no good candidates out there.

We found there are three secrets to building the team you desire and not leaving success up to chance:

1. Take the time to do it right.
2. Get to know yourself first, then get to know your team.
3. Know what you need—stop hiring the right people for the wrong job.

Secret 1: Take the time to do it right.

I want to say this again because I think it bears repeating: fifteen interviews. Take a minute to think about this rule. How does it make you feel? What is your mind saying to you? My guess is it's saying, *Marty's crazy. There is no way we can take that much time to build our team.* Here's my question back to you: How much time do you lose when you have to get rid of a bad team member?

At Advoco, we realized a long time ago that a bad hire can set us back years. Think about how much time you spend with a bad team member, what it took to recruit and train them, and how long it takes before you finally make a move to let them go. Dave Ramsey says that his company tries to hire "thoroughbreds," but sometimes a "donkey" slips through. It's going to happen, and no hiring process is going to be perfect. But leaving it up to chance is, well, stupid.

Think about this math. You have six people on your team and one is a bad hire. That's 17% of your team. Now, if you have one hundred people at your company and one is bad, it doesn't really seem like it sets you back. But if you follow the rule of thumb, you should have a leader for every six to eight people. So at least one entire team is severely impaired by your bad hire.

And if you're not being intentional about your hiring, it'd be a miracle to only have a 1% bad-hire rate. With just four bad hires out of one hundred, 24% of your teams are limping along. And if you've got 10% turnover—which is considered really good right now—you're making ten bad hires out of one hundred. That means about ten out of seventeen teams (six people per team) are impaired. That's 59% of your teams! Every time another donkey slips through, another team is operating well below its potential.

When you slow down the hiring process, you up your odds of making good hires. It takes time for you to know if a candidate is the right fit. And it takes time for the candidate to know if your company is the right fit for them. Relationships can't be built in a couple interviews or a couple weeks. You're not going to get a sense of who your candidate really is that quickly. And let's be honest—people have mastered the art of the interview. They know what to say and what not to say. They've done their homework, and they're going to appeal to your ego by talking about how great your company is. It's like dating—in the early stages, we'll say the things that keep us in the hunt.

When you slow the process down, you start to get a true sense of who the person is and what makes them unique or special. Sometimes that leads to really hard decisions. At Advoco, we spent a lot of time with candidates, and when you do that, you start to like a lot of them. And when you like people, you want to hire them. But here's where things got tough: We also started to learn why they weren't a good fit for the job. So as much as we liked them, we couldn't bring them on board.

In other cases, the long hiring process made our decision super easy. Over time, a candidate's true colors started to show, their mask fell off, and we got a glimpse of who they really were.

When the Mask Falls Off

At one point, we were in the process of looking for a technical resource. We just lost one of our best guys, and we were in a bit of a jam. Like I did with most of our recruiting processes, I put on my personal social media pages that we were looking for a senior technical resource.

Well, one of my former colleagues answered my post and said his son was looking for a new gig and that he might be interested in applying. After talking with him, we started the process. This person was well-spoken, sharp, and knew coding. He appeared to be a great fit, but there was something that was a bit off.

With all our candidates, we told them up front about our hiring process—it's long and could be a bit tiring, but ultimately we're trying to find the right fit for them and us.

While this candidate agreed to the process, I think he took offense to the continued interviews we were putting him through. Yes, I liked him and so did others, but there still seemed to be something off. And when we went to schedule the sixth interview, it came out.

Instead of accepting the sixth interview, the candidate asked us if we were going to hire him or not. He was a busy person, and he did not have time for all these interviews. Well, guess what. We got our answer. We told him we understood he was a busy person, but this was our process and if he wanted to withdraw his name, we would understand.

Later that afternoon we received a multipage letter from the candidate berating us about not hiring him and that our process cost us his services. Whew, we dodged a bullet. On top of that, I received an email from his father telling me how screwed up our hiring practices were, and if we didn't change, we would go out of business.

By sticking to our principles and our process, we weeded out a bad hire and saved ourselves a lot of time and money. If we'd brought this guy on, he wouldn't have fit our culture, and we would've had to replace him eventually.

This was a big lesson to the team and me in understanding the power of slowing down. Sure, it hurts as a leader to not be able to get someone to fill a role, but nothing hurts more than bringing in a team member that does not fit. We kept a donkey out.

Secret 2: Get to know yourself first, then get to know your team.

When I say "get to know" yourself and your team, two questions pop up. First, what are you trying to know? You're trying to learn how you and your team members communicate, how you all tend to operate in a professional setting, and what type of work you're best suited for. So, this isn't "get to know" in the sense of where people are from, their favorite movie, and how many kids they have—though that stuff is important too. This goes much deeper. The information you're looking for will help you build strong, highly functioning teams.

The second question that comes to mind is, how do you learn this information? You need the right assessments. There are lots of workplace personality assessments available—Myers-Briggs, Enneagram, The Big Five—but the two that I think are the most helpful are the DISC and the Working Genius. We'll discuss both of these below.

One more thought here: You need to get to know yourself first before you start assessing your team. That means, of course, you'll take the assessments that your team takes. But more than that, it means diving deep into your results and trying to understand who you are and how you tend to function. That will help you in countless ways as you interact with and build your team.

You also need to understand the assessment as a whole. That way, you can properly evaluate each team member's results. If you don't have a deep knowledge of the assessment, you won't be able to properly use the information you're getting. And it's that info that will help you build stronger, healthier teams.

The DISC

When I signed up for Ramsey's EntreLeadership conference, they emailed us something called the DISC personality assessment. They wanted us to take this test before the conference so we'd have our DISC profiles ready when they talked about them on day one. I'd taken personality profiles before, but the last one was probably in high school, and I think it said I should be a hairdresser.

The DISC profile is a personality assessment tool that helps people understand their behavioral tendencies and communication styles. It is based on the theory that people have four primary behavioral styles: Dominance (D), Influence (I), Steadiness (S), and Conscientiousness (C).

Here's a brief overview of each style:

Dominance (D): People with a dominant style tend to be assertive, decisive, and results-oriented. They like to take charge and can be competitive and direct in their communication.

Influence (I): People with an influential style tend to be outgoing, social, and persuasive. They like to be around people and are skilled at building relationships and influencing others.

Steadiness (S): People with a steady style tend to be cooperative, patient, and reliable. They are team players who prioritize harmony and are good listeners.

Conscientiousness (C): People with a conscientious style tend to be analytical, detail-oriented, and cautious. They value compliance, accuracy, and quality and are often seen as precise and methodical.

Okay, simple enough. So, I took the assessment recently and here is what my results looked like.

Marty's Results

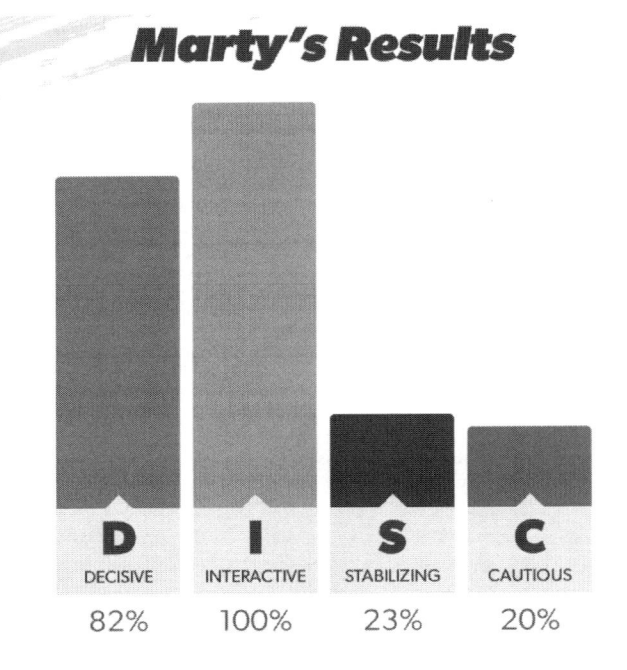

D	I	S	C
DECISIVE	INTERACTIVE	STABILIZING	CAUTIOUS
82%	100%	23%	20%

As you can see, each score is put on a bar chart so you can easily see where you stand in each category. Each style is scored on a scale of 1–100—the higher your score, the more likely you are to behave in a way that reflects that style.

Now, one thing to remember with a test like this: There is no right or wrong answer or perfect personality. You're not failing if you get a 1, and you're not crushing it if you get a 100. The DISC is just assessing your tendencies. I'm mentioning this because we are so conditioned by our years in school that we believe 1–100 is tied to grades, like A's, B's, C's. That's not the case here.

Here are my scores:

- D – 82
- I – 100
- S – 23
- C – 20

So what does this mean?

DOMINANCE (D)

Let's start with D. D is Dominance, and this means the higher on the scale you go, the quicker you make decisions. Doesn't mean they are right or wrong, just fast. With me being a high D, I usually don't require a lot of detail to make decisions, and my tendency is to jump fast.

For example, say you send me an email. In most cases, I have already made my mind up after the first paragraph. If you send me a 100-word email, my guess is I won't read it all, and if I do, I shut down at about word twenty. High D's are good to have on the team since you want to move forward, but to counterbalance that, you need people who are lower D to slow things down. They want more information, and they like to take their time.

When it comes to my leadership, I've already mentioned that the feedback I get from my team is that I'm moving too fast. That makes a lot of sense considering my DISC profile. Again, what's great about information like this is there's no right or wrong personality type—it just shows what a person's tendencies are.

When you think about assessments, they work in two directions. I get to know what my tendencies are, which helps me be more self-aware. And I get to see what other people's tendencies are, which helps me understand how to work and communicate with them. If someone is a low D, then I know I need to provide them with more information. If someone is a high D, then I know I need to be brief.

Here's another example of my DISC profile in action. My wife and I had friends who were expecting a baby. One day my buddy called to tell me his wife had the baby and all was well. I congratulated him and told him I'd pass the news on to my wife.

Later that day, I told my wife—who, by the way, is a low D—about it. You can imagine how that conversation went:

"That's great news! Is it a boy or a girl?"

Pause. "I don't know."

"Well, what's the baby's name?"

Pause. "I don't know."

"How much did the baby weigh?"

"I don't know."

"Don't you know anything? How'd you not ask about any of that?"

Then I sheepishly say, one more time, "I don't know."

But I do know. I'm a high D!

INFLUENCE (I)

Yep, I'm also a high I. When you look at my leadership style, it was driven by interacting with people. I love to cast vision and then share it with the team. As I talked about earlier, I love a good idea and I want to persuade people to adopt it. The downside of high I's is we can come across pushy. Guilty.

High I's are also extroverts. And you know what that means: I can't leave a party. We get really bad FOMO, we like to be involved with people, and we don't like to be left out. Now that's not a bad thing unless your wife is a low I like mine. Low I's tend to be introverted. You can hear the conversation now when we head out for a dinner party or a company event:

"Are we going to stay out all night?" my wife asks.

"No, no, I promise—just a couple drinks. We'll say hi to everyone, and we'll be out the door."

As you can imagine, we're one of the last to leave, and my wife is now mad at me. But we found an excellent solution to this problem: two cars.

STEADINESS (S)

They say someone with a high S is like a golden retriever—friendly, dependable, a person's best friend.

Typically, high S people like to work in teams, and if they're assigned to a project, they'll usually want to know who they'll be working with. Low S people like to work more independently.

At Advoco, we relied on a person's S score when assigning projects. If a person had a high S, we'd put them on collaborative projects. If they had a low S, we'd assign them to things that allowed them to work more independently. Of course, that didn't mean we just left them to themselves. They knew they could reach out to anyone on our team for help. But we did respect their preference for working independently—that's when they did their best work.

CONSCIENTIOUSNESS (C)

I like to also think of this one as *compliance*, and it's one of my favorite traits—probably because opposites attract. I'm very low C and only score a 20 here.

High C people tend to be detailed rule-followers. You know the person who looks at a PowerPoint slide or an email and the first thing they notice is a grammar or spelling error? Yes, this person is a high C.

What I love about high C's is they are thorough—nothing slips past them. Every organization needs people like this. If everyone had my C score, things would get sloppy. I was definitely the person misspelling words on PowerPoint slides.

You need both types of people when building a team. If everyone is a low C, then lots of projects get started, but not a lot get finished. Or if they do, they ship too quickly. If you have all high C's, then it takes forever to get projects started and even longer to get them done. The high C's will always want to polish up one more thing before they ship.

When you look at my DISC profile and my business partner's, we were totally opposite. I was a high D, he was a low D. I was a high I, and he was lower. We were very similar on the S, but when it came to C, again, we were totally opposite.

Now, you might want to know how it works out when you have two partners in a company with very different personality traits. I'm here to tell you it worked out great. The key to building a great team is to make sure you have different traits, views, and working styles. I like to be the idea person and move fast. My partner Steve was the counterbalance to that.

Key 2: It's Your Team—Don't Leave It to Chance

He would slow me down and make sure we thought through what we were going to do, and he made sure all the right pieces were in place. Let me give you an example of how this works.

As part of my role as head of sales and marketing for Advoco, I was responsible for bringing business in, and then Steve would lead the delivery. Part of that process involved RFPs (requests for proposals). Basically, a prospect would send us a list of requirements that they're looking for in a solution, then we'd have to respond in writing how we'll meet the requirements. As you can imagine, it requires a lot of detail and writing.

While I could provide the foundation and framework for how we wanted to respond, I hated to do the writing. That's where Steve came in. He was the detail guy. Steve's proposals were always amazing—proper wording, proper grammar, every question thoroughly answered.

So, I'd be writing a proposal and it'd be killing me—I'm low C, I just want to get this done—then at some point in the process I'd say, "Hey Steve, can you just take a look at this?"

"No, Marty. I know you're gonna want me to do all the work."

"Steve, no, no, no, I'm just worried about grammar. Just take a look."

"Alright, fine. I'll give it a quick spit and polish." Then what would happen? Steve would rewrite the whole thing. He had to. He couldn't let it go.

Now, was I using Steve's high C for my benefit? Maybe. But the truth is, he did amazing work. I couldn't imagine where we would have been if we didn't have him cleaning things up before they went out the door. That's a great example of how different personality types complement each other and produce stronger work.

One last thought about the DISC and how we used it. We had every hiring candidate take the DISC—that way we knew if they'd be a good fit for their role, and if they'd complement the team they'd be working with.

We also required everyone in the organization to display their DISC profile on their desks. So when you worked with another person, you understood their tendencies—how they liked to communicate and work. Doing that goes a long way in preventing conflicts and misunderstandings.

Working Genius

The other personal assessment we used is called Working Genius. It was created by Patrick Lencioni, best-selling author and president of the consulting firm The Table Group. Lencioni is known for creating models and methodologies that help companies improve team performance, leadership, and organizational health.

Lencioni developed the Working Genius framework out of his own personal frustrations at work. He found that certain kinds of work drained him—even kinds he was naturally good at—and he wanted to understand why. As he began exploring why this might be the case, he discovered some simple ideas: We all have God-given talents that bring us joy, and we all have tasks that frustrate us. When you do the work that gives you joy, it energizes you and you're effortlessly more productive. When you do the work that frustrates you, it drains you and you quickly run out of steam.

Lencioni identified six types of "genius" that individuals can bring to their work: wonder, invention, discernment, galvanizing, enablement, tenacity.

We'll explore each below. But first, I want to explain how the assessment works. It tells you a few things. First, you learn your two "working geniuses." These are the types of work you're not only great at, but you're also energized by. Then you learn your two "working frustrations." These are the tasks that drain you—even if you're good at doing them. Lastly, you find out your "working competencies." These fall in between your geniuses and frustrations. You're good at these kinds of tasks. They don't quickly drain you, but they don't energize you either.

What I like about this assessment is that it's not based on personality, but on how you work. It tells you what type of work gives you life and what type will completely drain you. This helps people understand where they can best contribute in the workplace and ensures teams have a balance of these geniuses so they can be more effective.

I also like that Working Genius is an interdependent model, meaning that teams need each kind of genius to function optimally. Once we understand that, we can celebrate our differences rather than judge people for not being like us. We need their unique geniuses to get the job done.

When you look at the six geniuses, there's a flow to them. They start with an idea—someone *wonders* if something is possible. Then someone starts to *invent* solutions for how this idea could become reality. Next, someone *discerns* if the idea is any good. If it is, you need a *galvanizer* to rally the team behind the idea, and then you need the *enablers* who like to say yes to things and are willing to help. Finally, you need people with *tenacity*—they'll get things done and push the idea over the finish line no matter what.

Let's talk in more detail about the six geniuses and what they mean.

Wonder

Wonder is the natural gift of pondering the possibility of greater potential and opportunity in a given situation. A person with the gift of wonder might be known as the person with their head in the clouds. They're always wondering *what if*. They challenge the status quo, and they can easily imagine how things could be better. These people are helpful because every new idea starts with wonder. You need someone to think, *Why do we do things this way? What if we did this instead?*

Patrick Lencioni shares a good example of what wonder looks like at the corporate level: While Walmart was worried about building bigger parking lots, someone at Amazon was thinking, *What if we didn't have any parking lots?*

Invention

Invention is the gift of creating original and novel ideas and solutions. People with this working genius love to invent and create. They'll hear the question that the wonderer asks and start figuring out a solution. Or they'll create something new out of nothing. Everyone has a little bit of this in them, but when this is someone's genius, they would rather create something new than do anything else. They're itching to find new ways to do things, and they don't want to do them how they've already been done. You need this type of genius in every area of your organization—from marketing to sales to engineering. Inventors come up with the brilliant idea and other team members work to implement it.

Discernment

Discernment is the gift of intuitively and instinctively evaluating ideas and situations. This is a unique skill. People with the genius of discernment are very good at connecting dots and seeing patterns. They can look at the inventor's new idea or solution and decide if it will work. They often operate on an intuitive level—they just have a sense of what will work and what won't.

Galvanizing

Galvanizers have the gift of rallying, energizing, and inspiring others to take action and embrace ideas. They love to encourage others and mobilize the team behind a new idea or solution. This is the genius you need if you want to get something up and running or if you want to sell something. Galvanizers are easy to spot—they're usually the ones who are talking the most.

Enablement

Enablers provide encouragement and assistance for an idea or project. I like to call this group "the people pleasers." They volunteer for everything and want to help as much as possible. When the galvanizer sets out the plan to tackle something new, enablers are the first people to jump on board. This category is probably the largest one we see in organizations, and without them I'm not sure much would get done. We just need them to say no every once in a while so they don't burn out.

Tenacity

Tenacity is the gift of pushing projects or tasks to completion to achieve results. This is the genius that I think gets the most discussion. I like to say a person with the genius of tenacity loves a good checklist and the last 20%

of any project. A quick way to find out if someone's genius is tenacity is to ask, "How do you feel about checklists?" If they get all wide-eyed about that, then you've got your answer. These people love knocking out to-do lists, and they don't rest until the job is done. As you might have already guessed, this is not one of my geniuses. I love to start a project, but I struggle to complete it.

You can imagine what this is like around my house. Every time I start a project, I get about 80% done and hit a wall. My tools will be laying around, and my wife eventually asks, "Are you going to finish this anytime soon?"

Now, I know what some of you high achievers are thinking, *I can do all of the working geniuses. I'm able to come up with an idea, implement it, and carry it over the finish line.* And yes, you probably can, but that's not really the point. The assessment helps you identify the two areas where you're not only the strongest, but where you feel joy and get energized by the work. As one of my colleagues used to say, these areas "give you the juice." When you stick to them, you'll be the most productive and efficient, and you'll be able to maintain a strong working pace for the longest amount of time. The assessment also identifies which working areas to avoid. When you let someone else do the work in those areas, you'll be less frustrated and less likely to burn out.

As I mentioned, tenacity is one of my working frustrations. So you know what I did in my organization? I made sure I always had people on my team with tenacity who love to get things done. They could take my ideas and make them happen.

When I wrote this book, I did the same thing. You can imagine the frustration I had trying to finish it. It was easy to come up with the idea, say I'd write a book, and start writing. But finishing it? No, no, no. So when I set out to hire a writer to work with me, I sent them the Working Genius assessment. They had to have tenacity or it was a no-go. See how this works?

Let me share with you another example of the Working Genius in action.

My daughter, Jamie, is a super creative person. In college, she majored in Visual Creations, focused on graphic design, and became an expert in all the design tools from Adobe's Creative Cloud. Her first job out of school was helping me build a website and all the visual elements of our marketing program. She then went to work for Ramsey Solutions as a graphic designer, creating sales and marketing ads. But over time, I could see she wasn't happy. Eventually, she moved over to their Live Events team as an event planner, and I saw the excitement return to her work.

It didn't make sense to me because she was so good at design. One day I had her take the Working Genius test, and I knew exactly what was going on. Jamie had the geniuses of discernment and enablement. This made sense because she's so good at connecting dots and seeing the correlation of things going on in the business. She's also a people pleaser. She loves helping people, and you rarely heard her say the word no.

Her working frustrations—invention and wonder—are what surprised me. How could a graphic design person not like inventing? But that was the problem. Just because we are good at something doesn't mean it brings us joy. For Jamie, the act of having to create and invent over and over was not something she liked to do. Inventing brought her frustration and anxiety, and if she could avoid it, she would.

If she could have taken the Working Genius assessment earlier in her career, it could have helped her get on the right path faster. It would have helped whoever hired her too—they would have known if the job was right for her. When you're hiring, you'll meet a lot of good, quality people, but are they the right person for the role and the team you're trying to build? It's not enough to find out if they *can* do the job, you need to know if the job gives them joy. And if it doesn't, then you're going to struggle as you lead them.

The Team Map

One of the standout features of the Working Genius framework is the Team Map provided by The Table Group. This map offers a clear, one-page overview of your team's strengths (working geniuses) and weaknesses (working frustrations). It's an invaluable tool that quickly shows what energizes your team members and what drains them. With just one glance, you can see how each person fits within the team, identify areas of strength, and pinpoint any gaps.

This insight is crucial not only for leading your team effectively but also for making informed hiring decisions. Often, companies unknowingly hire people who are just like them, which leads to an overemphasis on certain areas while neglecting others.

For example, I was working with a company and, after reviewing their Team Map, they immediately realized, "Wow, we don't have any inventors! We've all got the genius of either galvanizing, enabling, or tenacity." They were excellent at getting things done and supporting others but struggled with generating new ideas, which was a challenge they'd been facing.

Another interesting case involved a team leader who was strong in wonderment and enablement. This person thrived on brainstorming new ideas and was a natural people pleaser. However, when they shared their ideas with a team member who was strong in tenacity (someone who craves clarity and structure), things often went awry. The wonderer would come in excited with a new idea but lacking details, while the tenacity-driven team member would ask for clarity, which the wonderer couldn't provide. This led to frustration on both sides, and eventually, they began to resent each other.

After understanding the Working Genius framework, they realized the problem wasn't personal—it was about differing needs. By changing their communication style, they improved their interactions. For instance, the Wonderer could begin by saying, "I don't have all the details yet, but I'd like to run something by you. Could you help me think through what we might need to make it work?" This small shift allowed the wonderer to be heard while giving the tenacity-driven team member the clarity they needed. In the end, both felt satisfied.

The conversation also highlighted the need for diverse strengths. For an idea to be successful, you need a wonderer and inventor to generate it, a discerner to evaluate it, a galvanizer to rally the team, and enablers and people with the gift of tenacity to make it happen.

That's the power of the Working Genius framework and why the Team Map is such a critical tool for any leader.

What Do You Crave, and What Crushes You?

If you put in the time to understand Working Genius and learn your team's profiles, it will level up your leadership brand like you couldn't imagine.

And the real game changer is understanding what each working genius *craves* and what they're *crushed by*. Lencioni found that each working genius desires a specific kind of affirmation at work—this is what they crave. And each genius is demoralized by being treated a certain way—this is what crushes them.

For example, someone with the genius of wonder craves consideration. They're crushed when they bring an idea to someone and the response is, "Who cares?" They want someone to be open-minded enough to listen to them. If you quickly dismiss a wonderer, you'll deflate them.

Inventors crave freedom, and they're crushed by constraints. Give them space to operate and let them color outside the lines. If you say, "Just do it how it's always been done," you'll take the wind out of their sails.

Discerners crave trust, and they're crushed when someone says, "Prove it." Remember, these are people who connect dots and operate on intuition. A good example of this in the public sphere is a guy like Simon Sinek. He doesn't rely on a ton of research. A lot of his conclusions are gut-based. If Sinek's publisher wanted to crush him, he'd toss his next manuscript back and say, "Back all of this up with data." That's just not how a discerner operates.

Galvanizers crave a reaction. Good or bad—it doesn't matter. The worst thing to them is being ignored. They like rallying the troops, but they'll settle for a heated discussion with them instead. What they can't stand is the troops shrugging their shoulders and walking away without reacting at all.

Key 2: It's Your Team—Don't Leave It to Chance

Enablers crave appreciation. If you want to crush an enabler, don't acknowledge that they helped you. They're the ones you should publicly thank for their hard work.

The people with the genius of tenacity crave clarity. They want to know exactly what they should be doing and the steps to getting it done. They're crushed by ambiguity. They're the opposite of inventors who like fuzzy boundaries. The tenacious person wants hard lines.

Let me give you a real quick example of why knowing all this is so important. Let's say a couple of team members—one's an enabler, the other is a discerner—just worked their asses off on a tough project. So, you decide to shout them out publicly in a staff meeting.

The enabler loves this—it's all he needs. The discerner doesn't like this at all—he finds it condescending to just get a pat on the back. What would be the best way to let the discerner know you really appreciated his work? Sit down with him for ten minutes and listen to his opinions about the project, asking things like: How could we make it easier next time? What were the pain points? What went well? You can still shout him out, but listen to his ideas first. That's what the discerner craves.

As leaders, we have to realize that one-size-fits-all solutions don't work. Each team member is different. When you understand what makes them tick—what they crave and what crushes them—you can tailor your actions to that. That's how you keep them motivated and engaged.

Be careful about applying prescriptive advice that's supposed to work for everyone. I see this happen a lot—especially at large companies. As much as we want to streamline and make things simple, we can't always do that with people—they're complicated. What works for one person demoralizes another. You'll lose good people by not understanding who they are, what they crave, and what crushes them.

Secret 3: Know what you need—stop hiring the right people for the wrong job.

The last secret to building your team is to know what you need. This one might seem like common sense or like it goes without saying—of course you should know what you need! But when I talk to leaders, I don't get the sense they really know what they're looking for in a candidate. Yes, they put up a job description, but it's usually a description they've used over and over again. Or it's something they borrowed from another site or another company.

So, they have a sense of what they need in a candidate in terms of a certain level of experience, education, or certification. And of course they want to hire a decent, pleasant human being. But is that all it takes to get the right person? What does *right* mean?

In his best-selling book *Good to Great*, Jim Collins made his famous hiring analogy of getting "the right people on the bus."[1] His argument—which he backs up with research—is that leaders who took companies from good to great didn't do so by casting amazing new visions or strategies for their companies. Collins assumed that's how they would've done it—set the vision, inspire the team, and attract more talent. In other words, tell everyone where the bus is going, and they'll jump on.

Instead, Collins writes, "They *first* got the right people on the bus (and the wrong people off the bus) and *then* figured out where to drive it." I love this idea. In business, we focus too much on the destination and too little on the journey. If you've got the right people, you'll figure out where you need to go. And the opposite is true too. Collins writes, "If you have the wrong people, it doesn't matter whether you discover the right direction; you *still* won't have a great company. Great vision without great people is irrelevant."[2]

People often ask job applicants, "Where do you see yourself in five years?" I hate this question. I get that they might be asking just to see if the person is ambitious and forward-thinking, but the truth is, a lot of people actually think they'll be x, y, or z in five years—like it's a formula. But none of us has any idea. And it's the same in business. No one could have predicted the 2008 recession or the COVID-19 pandemic. Those events drastically derailed five-year plans at a global level. But if you were on a bus with the right people, you figured out what detours to take to

Key 2: It's Your Team—Don't Leave It to Chance

avoid disaster. And just as important: You had a good time doing it! Who you work with matters.

But as Collins notes, it's not just about getting the right people on the bus. They need to be in the *right seats*. I couldn't agree more. But Collins kind of leaves us hanging here. Who are the *right* people? And how do you get them in the right seats?

I think I've cracked that code, and it all goes back to knowing what you need. Here's the two-step process to getting the right person in the right seat:

1. Develop a PSF (Personal Success Factors) for each role.
2. Figure out which DISC and Working Genius profiles are necessary for the role.

Step 1: Develop a PSF.

PSF stands for Personal Success Factors. Some companies call these KRAs (Key Results Areas or Key Responsibilities Areas). You use a PSF to not only describe the job, but also what winning looks like in the role. You want a PSF to answer a few questions:

- What are we hiring this person to accomplish?
- How do we judge if they're successful? What would they need to do for us to say, "Yep, they nailed it"?
- What are their main tasks—things they can expect to do daily and weekly?

For instance, if you're hiring a sales manager, their PSF might be: "Implement strategies and systems to steadily increase sales year over year." They know that's their main objective. How they accomplish that will require them to create smaller, measurable goals. They might want to hire several all-star salespeople by a certain date, put the team through a proven training program, or rework the incentive program (or do all three!).

On a day-to-day level, the sales manager will be in lots of meetings with higher-ups and direct reports. When they're not in meetings, they'll be analyzing data, researching sales tactics and channels, and brainstorming better ways to motivate and coach the team.

You'll notice this role requires a certain set of qualities. It goes beyond experience and skills. For one thing, you need someone who loves and is energized by people. And that's exactly why you create the PSF—to find out who you need.

Then you'll use that information for the next step: comparing the PSF with the person's DISC and Working Genius results. A candidate might have the perfect resume and an amazing personality, but if what they'll be doing is in conflict with who they are, they're not the right person for the job.

Step 2: Figure out which DISC and Working Genius profiles are necessary for the role.

So, you've done the PSF and nailed down what the role requires—on the big-picture level and on the day-to-day level. Now, you need to find out what DISC and Working Genius profiles you need for that role.

Let's say you're hiring an editor, and you're using the DISC assessment. You'd want someone with a high C (Conscientiousness) and a low-to-mid I (Influence). Why? You need a very detailed rule follower (high C) who doesn't need a lot of interaction to stay energized (low-to-mid I) in their work.

For Working Genius, I'll give you an example of a hiring situation we faced at Advoco. We were looking for a marketing person, and we had two solid applicants. One was an art major, and her working geniuses tested as galvanizing and tenacity. That seemed pretty odd for an artist, so I asked her: "Do you like doing art?" She said, "No, not really. What I love is curating. Putting things together for an exhibition."

That made total sense. A tenacious galvanizer would be perfect for putting on an art show—but not for creating the art. An artist's genius would be invention.

The other candidate had the perfect resume. She'd started her own successful social media company. But she tested as an inventor and enabler. That is not the right profile for running a company. This ended up making sense too—the reason she was applying for the job was because she didn't want to keep running her company. It forced her to be tenacious, which drained her. What she should've done is hired someone with tenacity to complement her.

So, we've got two candidates for a marketing job that required a lot of repetitive work—reports and tasks that had to get done on a regular schedule. On paper, we should've hired the woman who'd run her own company. She's an entrepreneur who could get shit done, right? No, she actually lacked tenacity. And the artist? You'd think she was a head-in-the-clouds creator. But she wasn't—she was tenacious with both feet firmly on the ground. We hired the artist. Using the Working Genius assessment spared us from making the wrong choice and helped us make a great one.

That's what these tests do: They peel back the false self—the one in the interview who knows all the right things to say, the one with the perfect experience and resume—and reveal the true self. What was amazing about our hiring process is that candidates often walked away understanding more about themselves and what they should pursue next.

One last thought here. Make sure you're thinking about the whole team as you hire. You need balance. If no one on the team is tenacious, factor that into your hiring. You need that quality. If the team is heavy on tenacity, no one's inventing anything new. You get the idea. Look at the current team's profile and make sure your new hire complements the rest of the team.

Our Hiring Playbook

I want to give you a quick overview of our hiring process and how we used these tests. I don't want you thinking that you need to send every viable candidate multiple tests—that'd be time-consuming and expensive.

Here's what we did in our team-building process:

1. **Round 1:** Weed through resumes for twenty to thirty potential candidates.

2. **Round 2:** Send those candidates a video interview link (we used Spark Hire). We'd usually ask them six timed questions, and they'd get a minute to think about each question and then answer.
3. **Round 3:** Based on the video interviews, we'd narrow it down to five or fewer candidates. We'd then send those candidates DISC and Working Genius assessments.
4. **Round 4:** Based on the assessment results, we'd narrow it down to two or three people who would come for in-office interviews.
5. **Round 5 and beyond:** Start the long interview process (remember, we did up to fifteen interviews!).

I want to reiterate one more time that you do not personally need to do all of this. You're putting the systems and processes in place. Or if you're not a decision-maker for your company's hiring policies, you're using these principles and tests in your portion of the hiring process. So, maybe only your department or team uses these tests.

All of this ties back to intentionality. You're putting in the work on the front end to avoid lots of headaches and costs later. It's worth it. One of my best hires was a marketer named Mary, who later became known as Make-It-Happen Mary. I knew I lacked tenacity, and she had loads of it. We balanced each other out. I came up with ideas and she was happy to carry them out. That wasn't an accident. I didn't leave it to chance. I looked for someone with tenacity, and the assessments were crucial to finding her.

It's your team—don't leave it to chance.

Now, let's move on to Key 3: Understand the Power of Moments.

Chapter 7

Key 3: Understand the Power of Moments

Have you ever heard of the Magic Castle Hotel in Los Angeles? I hadn't until I read *The Power of Moments* by Chip and Dan Heath.

In the book, they tell the story about this fairly basic hotel that's rated number two on Trip Advisor in the whole city of LA. When you look at pictures of this place, there's nothing special about it. It's an old apartment complex from the 1950s. The rooms are fine. The pool is okay. You might even say some parts of it are below average—the lobby looks like a place you'd wait while you get your oil changed. So, what makes people rave about this place when they write reviews?

Well, next to the pool is a bright red phone attached to the wall with a sign above it that says, "Popsicle Hotline." When you pick up the phone, someone answers, "Popsicle hotline! We'll be right out." Then a person dressed like a butler—wearing a suit and white gloves—brings you a silver tray with popsicles on it.

Talk about a moment. Can you imagine what your kids would think of this? That's a story they'd be telling their friends when they got back to school. And it's all free of charge, with no limit to how many times kids can call for popsicles. The hotel does the same thing with snacks like Doritos and candy bars, board games, movies, and—for the parents—laundry. Yes, you can drop your laundry off in the morning and by the end of the day it'll be waiting in your room washed and folded. Not only that, it'll be wrapped in brown paper, tied with twine, and topped with a sprig of fresh lavender. Again, all free of charge.

How much do you think all of this costs? My guess is not very much—especially when compared to the value and joy it brings hotel guests. And whatever it costs, it's paid off. Almost a decade after Dan and Chip Heath wrote about this place, it's still rated one of the top ten best hotels in LA.

The Magic Castle Hotel understands how to harness the power of moments. But what exactly *is* a moment?

What Is a Moment?

I think we all instinctually understand what a moment is. To put it as simply as possible, a moment is something you never forget. It's unexpected. It's unusual. Your brain latches on to it because it's out of the ordinary.

Obviously, we don't just remember the good stuff—so moments can be positive or negative. But what you'll notice as we dig into this topic is that positive moments are always a result of intentionality. Negative moments usually lack intentionality.

How do you know if you've created a positive moment? There are three ways to tell if you're on the right track. You don't need all these to happen, just one is fine, but they're a good way to gauge if you've nailed it.

First, people start pulling out their phones and snapping pics (for instance, at a really awesome company event). Second, people can't stop talking about it—either right away on social media or later at work. Third, when people outside your company hear about the moment, their jaws drop and they say things like, "Who does that?!" That's the reaction we got at Advoco when we won the South Carolina Best Place to Work award. The host of the event was reading off the list of the fun things we did at our company, and he kept stopping and saying, "Who does this?"

Keep in mind, there's a flip side to all of these. People will have the same responses when a negative moment happens. For example, you might get the "Who does that?" response for all the wrong reasons. We'll see examples of that in this chapter. That's when you know you're on the wrong track. But with enough intentionality, that doesn't have to happen to you.

And let me say one more thing about knowing when you've created a moment: Sometimes you don't actually know. It sounds like I'm contradicting myself, but moments aren't always loud and full of fanfare. I've had people tell me years later about I time I quietly encouraged them, and they never forgot it. A lot of times I don't remember the incident at all. I was simply trying to be the best leader I could be for them. When you're intentionally trying to improve your leadership brand, you'll create these kinds of moments all the time.

The bottom line is this: As a leader, you're in a position to create lasting memories for your team—good or bad. I wouldn't leave that to chance. We'll see what happens when you do later in the chapter. We'll also see what happens when you're intentional and you tap into the power of moments.

When you choose to shape moments for your team, you'll see amazing—and often unintended—benefits. What these moments might look like is only limited by your imagination. But I do want to share some best practices on how to make the most of your moments.

Add Some Magic

Moments need magic. That little bit of oomph that interrupts what's expected and elevates it. The Popsicle Hotline is a great example. You're expecting to relax with your family by the pool—which is already a positive thing. But that red phone on the wall makes it a little magical.

A friend of mine went to a restaurant in Paris once. Just a random place he and his wife walked past late at night as they were recovering from jet lag. While his wife asked the hostess about a table, the bartender handed my friend two shots of a citrus liquor—a welcoming gesture that went beyond the mundane. But what came next was full-on magic.

When his wife came back, she said, "Our table is through that door." They got to the door and my friend looked around. "You sure it's this

Key 3: Understand the Power of Moments

door?" They were standing in front of an armoire. "I think so," his wife said. They opened the door and, sure enough, they were looking at coat hangers and a clothes rod. Just an armoire. But his wife persisted—"The hostess pointed at *this* door." They pushed on the back of the armoire and it opened, revealing a large, packed dining room strung with overhead lights. Were they inside? Outside? In Narnia? It was disorienting and unexpected. Magic.

So, how do you create these kinds of moments as a leader in a business setting? To understand how to add magic, you have to have an understanding of the mundane—of what's expected. In *The Power of Moments*, they call it "breaking the script."[1] People have an expectation for how events will unfold. To break the script—to add magic—you must defy those expectations. It doesn't have to be an expensive, complicated thing. A restaurant owner in Paris placed an armoire where a doorway would have stood. That's not complicated or expensive. My friend thought a hostess would show him to his table—he *expected* pleasant, mundane service. Instead, he and his wife were hit with magic—and a lifelong memory.

Chip and Dan Heath polled executives at a bunch of well-respected businesses in the service industry. They estimated that they spent 80% of their time eliminating negatives.[2] What does this mean? It means they're spending almost all their time making sure you have a smooth, pleasant experience. That might sound commendable, but to say it another way, they're making sure everything is mundane. And they're spending almost no time trying to wow you.

Consider this: When you drive for five miles on a road with no potholes, are you wowed? Is it memorable? Or do you not even think about it? Now, it takes a lot of work to get that road nice and smooth. There's no doubt about that. But smooth is the expectation. Lots of potholes would make us angry. No potholes doesn't even register. And it's the same in the service industry. A rude hostess would jar us. The script is broken. But a pleasant hostess is mundane. It's nice—but there's no magic.

A few years back at Advoco, we told our team that if revenue went up 20% in the next year, we'd take the whole company to the Caribbean. To keep the team updated on our progress, we wanted to do something unique. So, we put one of those big fundraising thermometers in our lobby. You know the kind—you color in a little more as the total goes up. Well, we wanted more magic than that. So our thermometer was a giant piña colada. It sat in sand next to some bare feet. As revenue went up, the piña colada went down. If it got to the bottom, we were off to the islands.

Was the trip itself exciting enough? Sure! But why not add some fun as we tracked our progress? A piña colada thermometer is Insta-worthy. It made our team smile. It's a little bit of magic.

When to Make Moments

There are three situations when leaders should be intentional about creating moments: during transitions, at milestones, and at times when someone is struggling or suffering.

Transitions

Transitions are moves from one stage of life to another—situations where there's a before and an after. Marriage is a good example—you go from single to husband or wife. A first day at work is another transition. You're transitioning from your old job to your new one, from not being a team member to being a team member.

At Advoco, we did our best to make the first day of work memorable. First of all, we eliminated potholes—meaning we made sure we were ready for you. Someone was waiting at the door so you didn't walk in awkwardly, wondering where to go. Your laptop was charged, your email was set up, your desk was clean and like new. We provided lunch too. That's the bare minimum that should be happening. Beyond that, we had tons of Advoco swag waiting for you, including a backpack, just in case you didn't bring a bag and couldn't carry all that new swag home. We wanted to communicate the idea that we weren't just prepared for your arrival, we were also excited about it.

Key 3: Understand the Power of Moments

I remember hearing about a company that only onboarded people on Fridays. The last thing they did before new team members left was to hand them a $100 gift card to a local restaurant. They told them to celebrate their new job over the weekend on the company's dime. That's magic.

Unfortunately, I've heard a ton of stories where companies offer no magic on that first day. They even miss the mark on the mundane—and things turn miserable. A buddy of mine went to work for corporate side of Chick-fil-A. He showed up, and they told him his laptop was backordered. Was that the end of the world? No, but it communicates to the new team member that they're an afterthought: "Oops, we forgot you were coming."

I heard another story from a friend about taking a job with a nonprofit organization. When they took him to his cubicle there was a half-burned-out light overhead and an old desk inside. On the desk was his work computer—a small tablet with a tiny foldout keyboard. The icing on the cake: The keyboard was covered with orange Cheeto dust. And the tablet was propped on top of a cardboard box—he guessed that was their way of making it a little more ergonomic. *Who does that?!* He quit the next day, wisely realizing it could only go downhill from there.

Forget magic, that took a turn to miserable. I understand that nonprofits have tight budgets, so I could forgive the tablet computer and the old desk. But there's no reason why a light bulb can't be changed and a keyboard can't be cleaned. And the cardboard box has got to go.

That first day with a new team member is an opportunity. Make sure they feel welcomed. You do that by being prepared for them. Have their tools, software, company logins, and physical space ready and waiting. And find a way to create magic. The script says they'll have a long, relatively exhausting day taking in a new culture, new processes, and new people. How can you break that script? How can you make it memorable and energizing instead of exhausting? Use your imagination and have some fun with it. You're setting the tone for the rest of their time at your company.

Milestones

A milestone is an accomplishment or achievement. A five-year work anniversary. Finishing up a long-term project—like a book or a new product launch. Buying a home, having a baby, anything that could be celebrated. Milestones are great times to create moments.

At Advoco, anytime a team member had a baby, we sent them a tiny Advoco onesie. Or if they bought a house, we made sure to send them a housewarming gift. It's important to acknowledge big moments in your team members' lives. And you don't have to be Oprah—"You get a car! You get a car!" A simple gift is perfect. A bottle of wine does the job.

When we had our first million-dollar month, we gave everyone a $100 bill and a handwritten note of gratitude from our top leaders. Simple and unexpected. When our team increased revenue 20%, we celebrated that huge milestone by taking everyone to the Caribbean. We shut down the company, invited spouses and significant others, and treated them all like kings and queens for a week. Okay, I realize that's Oprah-level, but in some cases you *should* go big if you can. Boost morale. Have some fun. Celebrate and bond as a team.

An unintended effect of this was how much it helped our recruitment efforts. When the up-and-coming engineers at Clemson University heard we took our interns to the Caribbean, they clamored to join our team. We had our pick of the brightest and the best, and we quickly became Clemson's number one co-op program.

When we took our recruitment efforts on the road, we got the same results. Our booth at Virginia Tech had a line out the door. The organizers asked if we would stay an extra two hours after the event closed to try and meet all the demand.

And as I already mentioned, we won South Carolina's Best Place to Work award two years in a row, which widened our applicant pool. People heard about our benefits and perks and events and thought, "Who does this?" That's when you want someone asking that question—when what you're doing is awesome. Not when you've got Cheeto-dusted keyboards.

Key 3: Understand the Power of Moments

Recently, I got a note from someone who worked at Advoco. He was thanking us for creating an exciting, fun place to work. Unfortunately, he was leaving after five years there. Things had changed since Advoco was acquired by a larger company, and he didn't like the direction it was heading. He told me something funny about how he got his job with us. He was a Georgia Tech grad, but he snuck into Clemson recruiting so he could interview with us. It worked! He bent the rules (okay, he broke them) because he'd heard how awesome our culture was. A little magic goes a long way.

Getting this stuff right just takes some intentionality. And if you're getting it wrong, it's probably because of a lack of intentionality. Let me give you an example.

I met a guy who runs a local company. We were talking about this book, and he said, "Man, I've got a story for you." His company was growing, and he had this amazing sales guy who'd been working on some big deals. One day, the salesman comes in his office and tells him he just closed the biggest deal in the history of the company. The owner looks at the salesman and says, "Okay, what's next?"

Wow. Who says that? *What's next?!* That's the response of a leader who had never thought about how to celebrate milestones. This leader knew he messed up. He told me he saw the wind go out of the guy's sails—completely deflated him. At least he knew he made a mistake, and I'm sure he'll never do it again. But what a missed opportunity for a moment. Unfortunately, it became another kind of moment—one the owner will remember as a huge leadership failure, and one the salesman will remember as that time his leader crushed him.

Prepare now for how you'd react in a similar situation. Think about what you'd do differently. "Let's pop some champagne!" would have been a good response. And get processes in place to celebrate predictable milestones—work anniversaries, promotions, births, etc. Be careful not to get too predictable though—that'll kill the magic. Mix it up from time to time. But don't get paralyzed wondering if you're being creative enough.

Doing something is better than nothing. I'm sure parents at Advoco knew we'd send them a onesie. It was still a nice, unique way to show that we cared.

Struggles and Suffering

It's fun to celebrate the good times, but you've got to show up in the bad times too. Don't let your team struggle or suffer alone. Find a way to help and show you care when bad things happen, like the loss of a loved one or a scary diagnosis. Even in less extreme situations—maybe their kids keep getting sick and their stress level is through the roof—acknowledge how hard that is and find a way to help.

I know of an office manager who no longer sends flowers when a team member is going through a tough time. She just doesn't see how that helps. So she sends food instead—gift cards to their favorite spots or a DoorDash card. Sometimes both. She knows firsthand that grocery shopping and cooking in the midst of a huge struggle can sometimes feel impossible. The executives at her company have empowered her to respond how she sees fit, and they trust her to represent the company well.

In these situations, focus on easing your team member's burden. Don't ask what they need from you—they likely can't even process what they need. Just make the gesture, buy the food, send the card, give them the days off. And allow them lots of flexibility in their schedule.

I recently heard a terrible story about a guy who had to quit because his company wouldn't budge on flexibility. He was a director in marketing who'd been with his company for years. Sadly, his father was diagnosed with a terminal illness and didn't have long to live. He asked his company if he could work remotely for a couple months to care for his dying father. They said no. They had a strict work-from-the-office policy, and they wouldn't budge. This guy—rightfully—quit. He knew what was more important. The company lost one its smartest, most effective marketing directors because they couldn't see that this was a moment—a chance to break the script and do the right thing.

Key 3: Understand the Power of Moments

What Moments Could You Create?

Let's take a few minutes to pause and think about how you could apply some of these ideas. Ask yourself: What moments could I create for my team? I've just got one rule: Focus on things you could implement within the next few weeks. We all like to daydream about what we'd do with an unlimited budget and no hoops to jump through. But in this case, aim for what you could reasonably get done in your current role. Don't stop dreaming about those big ideas. Just put them in your back pocket for now. You're looking for ideas you could act on almost immediately.

Remember, moments need magic. Think about how you could defy expectations and break the script. And think about when moments work well: when team members are in a transition, have hit a milestone, or are going through a tough time. Here are a few prompts to get ideas flowing:

- When new team members onboard, we could . . . (go to an arcade bar, buy them lunch every day for their first week)
- Employee X has had a really tough time lately, maybe we could give them . . . (a couple extra days of PTO, a day at the spa)
- My team nailed that big project recently and I missed the mark on celebrating, maybe I could surprise them with . . . (a bottle of champagne, an afternoon off)

Okay, your list might be way more creative than that, or you might steal a bunch of those ideas. Go ahead and write down moments you could create for your team or organization. And for a couple of these, feel free to think about a specific person who you could create a moment for.

Moments I Could Create for My Team or Organization

1. _____

_____

2. _____

_____

3. _____

_____

4. _____

_____

5. _____

_____

Now, some of you—probably the business owners—wrote down ideas and thought, *Damn, that's gonna get expensive.* I was in an EntreLeadership Mastermind group with other business owners, and we'd do monthly Zoom calls. On one call, we were tossing around ideas about how to boost morale, and someone mentioned providing free snacks and drinks. One business owner practically shouted, "They'll bleed me dry!" We all had a good laugh, but he was serious. The moral of this story is, don't jump to the negatives. If you only focus on how creating moments will hurt you, you'll never do any of them.

Would that business owner have been bled dry? Probably not. You'd get a couple people who'd take advantage, but most people are decent enough to do the right thing. Don't get scared by the what-ifs. You'll create budgets for these moments, and none of them have to be permanent things—you can do trial and error. And remember to have fun with it!

We often jump to worse-case scenarios without considering unforeseen positives. Remember that branded backpack Advoco gave people when they onboarded? That took on a life of its own that none of us could have ever imagined. Team members would take their Advoco backpacks on vacations, snap a pic of it, and post on social with the tagline, "Where in the world is the Advoco backpack?"

There's our backpack at the Grand Canyon, in front of Mount Fuji, at the Colosseum, at Buckingham Palace. That simple backpack became a culture-builder at our company. It's tough to put a price on that. So, just create the moment and see how it unfolds. My guess is you'll be glad you did. If not, shut it down and move on.

Moments That Moved You

One of the best ways to figure out how to create moments is to remember what moments were meaningful to you. For me, a couple stand out in terms of my career. Before I get to those, let me say that I enjoy big, fun get-togethers and the moments they bring. Remember, I'm a high I on the DISC assessment, so I love a good party—like Advoco's theme parties or its legendary Christmas parties. People still talk about those. So, when you're creating those big moments and events for your team, think about what you loved at different events, and pull in those elements.

But on a deeper level, I want you to think about moments that shaped who you are. Think about the meaningful moments when you had a shift in consciousness. When someone stepped into your life, made something click, and caused you to start moving in a different direction. Those moments usually happen in one-on-one conversations or they come from quiet time with an amazing book or podcast.

One of those moments for me happened in a meeting with Chris Oakley. Chris worked for Ramsey Solutions as the leader of my EntreLeadership Mastermind group. He was one of those special guys who just always knew the right thing to say, how to cut through all the BS, and how to help you get to the heart of the problem you were trying to solve.

In 2017, Chris left Ramsey to build his own consulting practice to help business owners win in the marketplace, but more importantly, to leverage their influence for the greater good of the world.

I was one of the first people to hire Chris to help me and my team learn how to be better—better leaders, better teammates, and simply better people. In our first meeting, Chris introduced me to Andy Stanley and his book *Principle of the Path*. In the book, Andy talks about how *direction*, not *intention*, determines our path in life. It's our daily choices that lead us to our ultimate destination. So, to build the legacy we want, we have to make choices that get us from where we are to where we want to be.

Chris went on to tell me that part of his leadership training required him to write his own obituary. So when he was twenty-eight years old, that's exactly what he did. That kind of blew me away. It's unheard of. *Who does that?!* You know it's a moment when someone stops and asks that question.

Now, I'm not sure where you stand on your own mortality, but this was not a subject I liked talking about. I wanted to talk about living—how to run a business and how I was going to be successful—not dying. I wanted to talk about all the great things I wanted to do with our company and where I believed we could go with it. But Chris said no. That the key to running a successful team and business had to start with who I am as a person, who I wanted to be, and what legacy I wanted to leave behind.

The reality is, we are only on this Earth for a short moment in time, and if we don't address our own mortality, then how do we know how to live our lives? As Andy Stanley says, "The direction you are currently traveling—relationally, financially, spiritually, and the list goes on—will determine where you end up in each of those respective areas."[3] Just like any journey, the only way to set the direction you want to go is to start with where you want to end up—the destination. That's why writing your own obituary is a powerful exercise. You're writing down what you want people to say about you when you're gone. And that will change how you choose to live today.

At twenty-eight years old, Chris knew his life mission. And he started living it. For me, this was a moment. A powerful moment. To think about who I wanted to be as a person and the legacy I wanted to leave behind.

How many of you have taken the time to write down who you want to be as a leader, a parent, a friend? What would you like to hear from your spouse, kids, friends, and colleagues when you're gone? I have yet to read one obituary that talks about what car a person drove or how many houses they had. No, they all talk about the person. Their actions and their effect on other people.

Memento mori is a concept that Chris brought to my attention. It's a Latin phrase that can be translated to mean "remember you will die" or "remember death." That thought isn't meant to discourage you. In fact, it should have the opposite effect—live better, live harder, pour yourself into every moment. After all, life is just a series of moments. Make them positive. Make them count. You never know the ripple effect they can have—even long after you're gone.

When Moments Become Movements

When I left Advoco, a member of my team named Mary (aka Make-It-Happen Mary), gave me a binder full of stories that people told about working with me. She also gave me a piece of word art. It was all the words people said about me and my leadership—words like *mentor, inspiring, friend, fun, passionate, positivity*.

I mentioned this already in chapter 2, but I'm bringing it up again because it was a huge moment in my life. And it was about more than just how incredible those gifts were. I got to witness the power of moments come full circle. I'd strived to make moments with my team count, and now here they were creating a moment for me. That's exactly what you want. Your team should move beyond just being the recipient of moments and start creating moments for others. That's the ripple effect, and you have no idea how far and wide it can reach.

Connect for Good

We all remember March of 2020. COVID-19 brought the whole world to a standstill. At the time, I was in Nashville meeting with a bunch of other small-business owners when news kept coming in about a possible pandemic. We were supposed to get together to talk about leadership and to evaluate how we were doing as leaders in our organizations, but it was tough to focus on that. We couldn't help thinking and talking about what we were going to do when we got home.

Were we going to figure out how to work in the office while keeping everyone safe? Were we going to shut down our businesses and send everyone home? These were the questions everyone was asking.

When I got back to Greenville, I remember vividly when we gathered our leadership team to make a final decision about what to do. Quite frankly, this was an easy decision for me as a leader: Everyone needed to stay home and stay safe. We had begun doing more and more remote work, so this was just that process on steroids. The bigger question for us at that time was about a customer conference we had coming up in five weeks. Should we shut it down?

Every year we held a conference called Connect. It was always the first week in May when the weather is just beautiful in Greenville, South Carolina. About four hundred people would attend, and we'd spend time getting to know each other and learning more about the software product our clients used.

For Connect 2020, we had hotels booked, a conference center ready to go, and a host of restaurants and caterers preparing to serve close to three thousand meals. What was going to happen if we have to cancel the conference? Every day this weighed on me and my marketing team. Emails were flying back and forth. Telephone calls were coming in, asking us what we were going to do. If my leadership brand was going to be tested, it was now.

After much discussion with clients, our team, and industry experts, we decided to have a virtual conference. I'm sure you know now what I'm

Key 3: Understand the Power of Moments

talking about, but this hadn't really been done back in May 2020. Tools were becoming available, like Zoom, but not many people tried to hold a three-day conference 100% online.

The good news was, we had been doing webinars and virtual meetings every month as part of our drip marketing strategy, so we had an idea of how to do it—just not at the scale of a conference. But we dug hard into one of our core values, courage, and we made it official: Connect 2020 was going remote.

Then it hit me. What about our signed contracts and financial commitments with local vendors? If we go virtual, it could cost us a fortune. One by one, I made the calls to our vendors. Marriott was first. They graciously let us out of our contract. They knew the predicament we were in, so they said let's just roll the contract over to next year. As I continued making calls, every vendor said the same thing. I don't think I have ever been prouder to be a businessperson in Greenville than I was that day.

The last agreement was the hardest. Not because of the money but because it was our local caterer. They were going to supply food for breakfast, lunches, and one of our evening activities. The part that made this so hard was not only that they weren't going to be able to serve food for the event, but all their restaurants also had to be shut down and all those people were being put out of work.

So, yes, this one was different.

The head of company was a man named Carl Sobocinski. He was a pillar in our community. Some say he saved downtown Greenville because he brought one of the first fine-dining restaurants downtown thirty years ago. That started a chain reaction that now makes downtown Greenville one of the coolest places in the US.

As part of the Connect budget, we had allocated $15,000 to the catering wing of Carl's restaurant group, Table 301. Since we didn't need those meals for the conference now, I wondered how we could use them to serve the community, and maybe provide a few jobs too.

So I gave Carl a call. I told him I didn't want to talk over the phone but would like to meet in person so I could share with him our plan for the money. Carl graciously agreed to meet with me at his restaurant but said we'd need to do it outside, socially distant. Deal.

My home is about a mile from his downtown restaurant, so I decided to walk. I'll never forget how quiet it was. With everything shut down, people didn't need to drive. I walked right down the middle of our formerly busy street.

I sat down with Carl and told him how we were moving our conference online. And I told him that we'd agreed to push all our other contracts to next year, but with him, I wanted to break the script and do something different.

I had $15,000 to spend with his company. I wanted to figure out how we could take that money and use it to feed people in the community over the next ten weeks. Now, I know it wasn't a lot, but I thought it would be a start and something our company could do to help. My marketing team had already come up with a name: Connect for Good.

My thought was, we could provide maybe two thousand meals to people in need.

My church, which is located downtown right next to a low-income housing complex called Towers East, had tried to provide support to the tenants over the years. But the building owner made it clear we weren't allowed on their property. The police had even been called on church members for trespassing.

So, the plan was to invite the residents over to the church once a month and provide them with a nice meal. Unfortunately, Covid hit and this plan had to be put on hold.

While talking with Carl, I wondered if we could create a box lunch. Then we could distribute them right at the property lines so we wouldn't be in violation of any trespassing rules.

Carl thought about it for a minute and came up with a menu. He'd put together a pimento cheese sandwich (for those of you not from the South

Key 3: Understand the Power of Moments

this is a southern specialty, and no one did it better than Carl's team), a bag of chips, fruit, and a cookie. It would be easy to transport as well as serve. It sounded like a great idea. I asked if he could make a couple thousand of these over the next two months.

Carl looked at me and said, "I want to be a part of this community service. What if I can do it for three dollars a meal?" I looked at him and this incredible warmth came over me. This was a moment. We set out to serve a couple thousand meals with the small amount of money we had, and instead we'd be able to serve five thousand meals.

Now I'm not sure if you're religious or not, but five thousand meals is a number all Christians know. For me, it was a sign—a sign that this Connect for Good thing was going to be special. I couldn't wait to get started.

We decided to run the program over fourteen weeks and hand out 350 lunches every Wednesday. I'm not 100% sure why we settled on this, but that was the plan. Carl's team would make the lunches on Tuesday night and our team from Advoco would pick them up and work with different groups to hand them out to people in need.

We were ready to go for our first Wednesday. We planned to hand out meals from my church's property to the people living in Towers East. I'd arranged with the pastor to have a team there, and we would bring the food to be handed out.

But on Tuesday, the mayor of Greenville made an announcement: Covid was getting worse and anyone caught gathering outside would be arrested. My pastor called me, "Marty, this is Pastor Susan. Did you see the announcement from the mayor?" I said, yes, I did. She said, "We cannot do the event tomorrow. I don't want to get arrested." Me being a bit of a jokester, I said, "Susan, think of the prison ministry we could start!" She didn't think that was too funny. I told her I understood, and we hung up the phone.

I thought, *What am I going to do with 350 meals?* I called Carl and told him the news. He said that they'd already made all the meals—they're boxed and ready to go. At this point, we have to use them. So, once again I said that I understood. I told him I'd try to come up with another idea.

Then it hit me. My neighbor works in the emergency room at the local hospital, Prisma Health. No one had been under more stress and tension than the ER team in our community. What if I could provide free meals to them?

So, I called my neighbor up and told her about the situation and how I would love to feed the doctors, nurses, and any support staff in the ER. She told me she thought that would be a great idea. She'd call some people to make sure it was alright. A half hour later, she got the green light. Her supervisor thought it was a wonderful idea and we were welcome to bring the meals tomorrow. Our first delivery was set to go.

The next day, we loaded the Table 301 vans with food and headed over to the ER. We handed them out to nurses, doctors, ambulance drivers, support personnel, and even the helicopter transport drivers. The smiles and joy these people shared with us was a feeling you can't ever forget. Yes, it was just a box lunch, but it was much more. We were adding some magic to the mundane. It was an acknowledgment that each and every person mattered. We all carry our own burdens and challenges, and for a moment, just sharing a box lunch said, "You matter, and we are here to celebrate it." That day was special for all of us, and we'll carry that feeling forever. But this was only day one, and we were just getting started.

When week two rolled around, the ban on outside gatherings was still in place, so we still couldn't feed our friends at Towers East.

I received a call from the other hospital in town who heard what we did for Prisma. They wondered if we could do something similar for them. I told them they were in luck because we were looking for a place to serve meals this week. So we fed their ER team, facilities team, security guards, and the team that was administering Covid tests to the thousands who drove in. All with the same message of gratitude and thanks for what they do for our community.

Key 3: Understand the Power of Moments

Word started to spread, and requests came in from all over the place. One of our next stops was the local soup kitchen. As we got talking with the director and her staff, we could see so much joy on their faces. What we didn't realize was that because of Covid, they were not allowed to have any volunteers help them. The director and her small team were responsible for making and serving meals every day all by themselves. By providing them with boxed lunches, they were able to take a break that day and get some sorely needed time off.

One of the nice touches our team added was to place short messages in with the meals so whoever opened the box got a note of hope and encouragement. And everyone needed it in that trying time. We wanted to create some small but meaningful moments for people.

As word kept spreading, people were asking to volunteer and donate money. The challenge was, we were not a 501(c)(3) charitable organization. I was not able to take money and give people a tax deduction. Any money I took in would be taxed, so less of it would go to the people we wanted to help.

That's when an old acquaintance from the nonprofit world, Dan Weidenbenner, volunteered to help us. He'd developed a mobile platform for fundraising. He set up a page for us where people could donate, and he would distribute the money. All tax-free and in compliance legally. Wow, the blessings kept coming.

So we set up the site, and the next month we raised another $60,000 from companies and individuals in the community who wanted to help.

Sixty thousand dollars! That meant we were able to serve another twenty thousand meals. By this time, we were up to over five hundred meals a week.

We were able to serve families living in temporary housing. We were able to serve homeless military veterans living in hidden tent camps. We continued to serve the soup kitchen and other agencies that just needed a break. We were able to meet some amazing people who just needed a gift of love through a meal and someone to talk to.

One story that just broke my heart was the day we fed the Greenville Police Department. After spending time with the amazing men and women in blue, the director came up to us with tears in her eyes. She said thank you for thinking of them. Unfortunately, during that time there was lot of pressure on the police, and they weren't able to eat in the community for fear of retribution. It was a tough situation for everyone, but even police officers needed to know they mattered. They're humans just like everybody else and need to know people care.

Finally, the mayor decreed we could gather outside again as long as we followed certain guidelines. So, we were able to feed our friends at Towers East. As each person came by, we shared a meal and a quick conversation. Every week we invited other members of the Advoco team and friends who donated money to share in the experience.

Another surprise blessing came from Dan, the same guy who created our donation site. He ran some community farms and a nonprofit that helped feed families, and he received hundreds of boxes of produce each week. He passed some of that on to us, and we were able to give out a bag of fruits and vegetables to the residents of Towers East each week. We really couldn't believe how things like this kept happening.

We were now in our seventh month of feeding people. What started out as a vision to provide two thousand meals had now hit the thirty-thousand mark. We'd met awesome people all over the community and been places we never thought we'd go, including Perry Correctional Facility, where we fed the incarcerated men on Christmas day. What a blessing and what a gift the world was giving us.

But things were about to get even better.

During one of our weekly calls, Carl (who ran the restaurant group Table 301) brought up that he heard our county was providing money through a program called the CARES Act. It was money from the federal government to help severely distressed sectors of the economy and provide aid to those people in need. What better program than Connect for Good? At the time there were not a lot of programs that met the criteria, so there was plenty of funding still left. The team decided to put in an application for $500,000.

At first we thought it was a crazy idea. We started this thing on a whim with a few thousand dollars, and now we might get half a million?

Within a matter of weeks, we were approved. The committee loved the work we were doing—not only helping families but also providing jobs to the restaurant industry that so badly needed the work.

Connect for Good had hit the big time.

We were so excited—this meant we were going to be able to serve another 150,000 meals. But then the reality set in. This was not a full-time job for any of us. We had a business to run in the midst of a full-on pandemic. This was going to require getting more restaurants and more people involved to make this happen. Plus, we'd learned that we were a little late to the CARES Act party. Part of our grant stipulated that we had to spend our money in the next six weeks!

Once again, Carl helped us out. This time we tapped into his team that coordinates the annual Euphoria food festival in Greenville. With the pandemic happening, this team was idle and looking for a way to be productive. So, they helped with planning, scheduling, and coordinating all the restaurants to prepare the meals and help with the delivery.

Each week we were doing up to five thousand meals. It was crazy. My original goal when we first started was two thousand total meals. Now we were doing more than double that every week. We were sending meals to school kids and families all over the place. We continued to serve the regulars that we were helping, but we needed to find even more groups. And we did. In fact, we were so successful in deploying the money that we were granted another $500,000 to finish the year.

When we totaled up the program at the end of 2020, we had raised more than $1.2 million and served more than 200,000 meals.

As I look back at my career, I can honestly say Connect for Good was one of my proudest accomplishments. To bring smiles to so many people and to have the ability to affect so many lives is something I will never forget. And it all started with a moment. We looked for a way to break the script—to give rather than receive. We wanted to add some magic to people's lives during a very scary and anxious time. And that moment led to thousands of others. People all across our area felt seen and cared for. Pretty soon, we had a movement on our hands.

When you embrace the power of moments, you'll eventually stumble on movements within your organization. It won't always be as dramatic as accidentally starting a nonprofit to feed the needy. But you'll see that when moments gain momentum, they become movements. This happens all the time at successful companies. The Popsicle Hotline is a great example—the owners tried out a unique, fun idea. Now, you've got people all over social media and YouTube filming themselves using that red phone to get a silver tray of popsicles. Then the Popsicle Hotline story ends up in a successful business book, and it's inspired thousands—maybe millions—of people to harness the power of moments.

In your own company, movements will often come from traditions that just started on a whim. Yvon Chouinard, the founder of Patagonia, wanted his employees to always have the chance to surf. So, they had surf reports posted in the office. If the conditions were good, anyone was free to go catch waves. This led to him writing a training manual for his company called "Let My People Go Surfing." That eventually turned into a book published in 2005. It's since been translated into ten languages and used in business colleges across the country. And the tradition of leaving work to surf lives on at Patagonia. When the weather is perfect, employees are free to go surf, bike, rock climb—anything that gets them outside.

In terms of your leadership brand, you get to decide what moments turn into movements. And what I meant by that is this: When you notice that certain moments are successfully working, you can turn them into things you do over and over again.

For instance, let's say you gave your team the afternoon off randomly one day after they'd finished a tough project. You noticed that it really boosted their morale. So, you tried it a few more times. It kept working,

Key 3: Understand the Power of Moments

so you kept doing it. And what's the value or philosophy behind that? Rest. Work hard, play hard. Whatever you want to call it, you've got the potential for creating a movement. And that can take many forms. You don't have to always go with the afternoon off. The larger idea is that breaking the script and promoting rest is a surefire way to create moments with your team. And when you lead your own company someday or have a seat at the decision-making table, you can push to make that a part of the culture. From there, you could end up with a movement.

So, here's my challenge to you: Break the script. Add some magic to the mundane. Be the leader who creates meaningful moments for your team. That's a fundamental key to becoming the leader people are happy to see.

Now let's get to the next key: Become a Learner.

Chapter 8

Key 4: Become a Learner

My favorite line from Harry Truman is, "Not all readers are leaders, but all leaders are readers."[1] Throughout my career, I've been known as *that guy*—the guy who reads all the time and has a book or story for every situation. The funny part is, I never liked to read as a kid. Why would I stay home and read when I could be out building forts or playing with friends?

This attitude toward reading carried over into school. I wasn't the best student—I got by with C's. And that carried over into college. I associated reading with memorizing stuff for a test. It was a means to an end. If I did read (and I did my best to avoid it), I found it painfully boring. That all changed in a moment in one of my business classes.

I remember so vividly sitting in class when the professor started telling a story about a company that went bankrupt. I perked up. *This was interesting.* It wasn't abstract. It wasn't a bunch of terms to memorize. It was a story about what business looks like in the real world. That made sense to me.

I spent hours reading and studying about that bankruptcy story. And when the test came, I aced it, right? No. Not one question was about the business's bankruptcy! I got my customary C. But I learned something about myself: I *actually liked* learning.

Key 4: Become a Learner

Why Learning Is a Superpower

The other day at the bookstore, I saw a sticker that said, "Reading is my superpower." I couldn't agree more. I love seeing stacks of books. It reminds me of all the cool things I have yet to learn. Nothing excites me more than the thought of where reading will take me—who I'll become, what I'll learn, and how much further ahead I'll be compared to where I am now. But you'll notice the title of this chapter is "Become a Learner," not "Become a Reader." That's because reading is only one way to learn. I do think it's an important one—we soak in knowledge better when we read.

But maybe you're listening to this as an audiobook and thinking, *Reading's just not my thing—never will be.* That's fine. Some of us gave up on books because we struggled in school. Let me tell you this: You can suck at school and be great at learning. And being a learner is the ultimate goal. A learner is two things: *curious* and *willing*. Curious about the world and willing to absorb new ideas and information. That's it. You can learn by going to conferences, having conversations, watching YouTube videos, and listening to podcasts and audiobooks. Reading is just one slice of the pie.

For me, it's my favorite slice. Reading is the most efficient way to take in information. I can crank that podcast play speed to 1.5x or 2x, but reading is still faster. So if you're not a reader, I'd encourage you to start incorporating reading into your routine. But again, it's not a necessity.

Whether it's reading or podcasts, the point is this: You have to keep learning. It's what will keep you in the game.

Here are a few reasons why you should make learning part of your daily routine:

- Learning gets you to the next level.
- Learning makes you more interesting.
- Learning helps you think differently.
- Learning is contagious.

Learning Gets You to the Next Level

When I first got out of college, I took a job as a salesperson. I'd never done anything like this before, and college doesn't train you how to do sales. So, my boss sent me to a Dale Carnegie sales training seminar. The class was held at a hotel, once a week for ten weeks. I learned a ton and still remember a lot of it, like the "sales burger," and the all-important opening line. For instance, "If there was a way for you to have an actual superpower, wouldn't you want to know more about it?" Wait for the inevitable, "Yes." "Good, well then let me tell you about reading."

My biggest takeaway from this course was that I was good at selling. I knew people. Would I have found this out eventually? Probably. But ten weeks in a windowless conference room at a Hampton Inn changed the direction of my life. It gave me the knowledge I needed to keep moving forward. That's the power of learning.

And I realized something else. That old quote was right: "What got you here won't get you there." A college degree is what got me that sales job, but that education couldn't help me in my new role. In other words, what got me here (college) couldn't get me there (success as a salesman). I had to be open to learning something new to get to the next level.

I've tried to be a learner ever since. Early in my career I was always on the road. I'd drive forty to fifty thousand miles a year. I spent that time listening to cassette tapes from the greats—Zig Ziglar, Earl Nightingale, Brian Tracy. I don't know if you remember those old cassette sets. You'd get six or eight tapes in this giant plastic case the size of an encyclopedia book. That was my version of Audible. Now, you've got all that knowledge on your phone. And most of it's free.

Soaking in the wise words of guys like Zig Ziglar propelled me to the next level in my career. If I'd just listened to sports radio on those trips—who knows—maybe I'd still be on the road fifty thousand miles a year.

I talk to a lot of leaders, and I'd say two-thirds don't make learning a priority. They know they should, but they usually claim they just don't have the time. I'm not going to guilt-trip them—they definitely *are* busy.

Key 4: Become a Learner

Between work and family and social obligations, they've got a lot going on. But when you dig in a little, you can find all kinds of time for reading and learning. Do you have a commute? Do you go to the gym? Do you do chores around the house? There's the time. Do you have a computer in your pocket that gives you access to all the world's greatest thinkers? There's your source of knowledge.

If you're ready to get to the next level as a leader, learn something new. Aggressively seek out new ideas and strategies and tactics. This doesn't mean you change your values. Those stay the same. That's the strength of developing your leadership brand—it gives you guardrails and keeps you focused on who you want to be. But everything else is fair game.

As the late Charlie Munger, Warren Buffet's longtime friend and business partner, said, "Keep learning all your life."[2] Why is this so important? Because the world never stops changing and your competition is always learning. You may be very confident in your abilities—and you likely should be—but you'll need to build on those to get to the next level. You can't stop and assume you've got it all figured out.

So, read the book, subscribe to the podcast, go to the conference—pop in a cassette tape if you have to. Just keep learning.

Learning Makes You More Interesting

When a leader who feels stuck comes to me for advice, the first question I ask is, "What're you doing to make yourself more interesting?" That might seem odd. But what I've found is that most people rely on the same predictable things to get ahead—work hard, follow orders, rinse, and repeat. There's a point, though, where kissing ass, doing what you're told, and being a hard worker won't get you noticed. You've got to bring more to the table and become one of the more interesting people in the room. And you do that by becoming a learner.

The reason this works is simple: If you're encountering new ideas, you've got more ideas to share. And if you're intentionally pursuing interesting things, that changes others' perceptions of you and your perception of yourself.

Here's a quick way to get started with this. Ask yourself two questions every day: What am I going to do to better myself? Am I more interesting today than I was yesterday?

Bettering yourself can involve a lot of things and go beyond just reading or passively taking in information. It could look like a new hobby: You're the gal who does jiu jitsu. You're the guy trying to become a master carpenter. Both of those involve a lot of learning. They signify you're open to new things and you're growing. And they're interesting.

When you start pushing yourself to grow and learn, that will inevitably show up at work. Interesting people get noticed. And beyond that, it's about living with some passion. Doing things you love. Learning things that challenge you. That's a big part of a life well lived.

You might find that your company doesn't reward this kind of thing. Well, maybe you're at the wrong place. That's another perk of learning and growing: You find out more about who you are and what you value.

Learning Helps You Think Differently

Remember the movie *Moneyball* with Brad Pitt? It's based on the true story of the Oakland A's 2002 season. The A's general manager, Billy Beane (played by Pitt), is devastated that the A's got beat by the Yankees in the 2001 playoffs. So, he starts thinking about what he could do differently. His main problem is he's working with a $41 million payroll, the second lowest in the MLB. In comparison, the Yankees' payroll is more than three times bigger at $125 million.

On a recruiting trip, Beane meets Peter Brand, a Yale guy with an economics degree. Brand talks about using something called *sabermetrics* to evaluate players. The term comes from the acronym SABR (Society for American Baseball Research), and it's basically a whole new way to see what kind of value a player brings to a team. It goes way beyond the usual stats, like hitting percentage and runs batted in (RBI).

Now, I want to mention the guy who coined this term *sabermetrics*. His name is Bill James, and he started toying around with these new ideas as a night watchman at a pork and beans factory in the 1970s. Sounds made

Key 4: Become a Learner

up, but it's 100% true. He published a small book about sabermetrics that sold seventy-five copies. So, that's the guy Billy Beane is basing his strategy on. And that matters because in one of the famous scenes in the movie, Billy Beane's colleague looks at him and says, "You're not buying into this Bill James bullshit, are you?"[3]

Of course, he was completely bought in. And he hit a lot of resistance trying to get people to use sabermetrics, but he stuck with it and built a team around these ideas.

In the end, the Oakland A's went on the longest winning streak in modern baseball history—twenty games. No one had even come close to that since 1977, when the Royals won sixteen games. Clearly, sabermetrics worked. The rest of the league took notice and scrambled to get these ideas in their organizations. Within a year, Bill James had a job as senior advisor with the Boston Red Sox. He worked with them for seventeen years and won four World Series with the team. The "Bill James bullshit" had turned into the Bill James gospel.

So, what's the moral of the story? Billy Beane, the industry insider, was open to new ideas and willing to learn. He broke the script and, in a way, committed baseball heresy by trying out some unorthodox ideas.

Now, this is interesting because the Oakland A's were not a bad team at the time—even with their meager budget. They had the second-best record in the league in 2001. So, sabermetrics wasn't some Hail Mary, we've-got-nothing-to-lose play on Billy Beane's part. He could have taken the well-traveled path, made some tweaks to the lineup, and just kept doing what he was doing.

And that's the deeper lesson here. If you were at the top of your game, would you be willing to throw out all your old methods and basically start from scratch? Or would you rest on your laurels, enjoy the success, and keep doing what you're doing?

Billy Beane could've done that. His already-successful career would have continued. Why did he take the risk on something different? He's a learner. Once he discovered promising new ideas, he couldn't let them go.

That ended up taking him from successful GM to legendary GM. But more importantly, he didn't take the safe, easy path, and he stayed true to who he was—a learner who thinks differently.

When you're continually taking in new information and ideas, you'll start connecting dots in new ways. And that will make you an incredibly valuable person to have around. So, keep learning and discovering. You never know when you'll stumble on the next big idea.

Learning Is Contagious

A friend of mine once had a leader who came to meetings completely unprepared. The team met once a week for an hour, and the meeting often devolved into whatever random thing had caught the leader's attention that day—so much so that the team started calling it "The Variety Hour." They never knew what to expect. Once, the leader spent a half hour reading a Twitter thread about a guy at a Waffle House. Another time, he spent half the meeting telling stories about his boss from the 1990s.

Now, none of this is bad in itself. If the purpose of the meeting was to blow off steam and bond, then it'd be fine. But there was no intentionality behind it. The team itself usually had an agenda—at least for a while. But the leader would sidetrack the meeting, and no one felt like they could call him out on it. So, they started coming unprepared too. It was just an hour to kill.

Here's what the leader was communicating: This meeting is not important. From there, it was a quick leap to: The work we do is not important. That attitude seeped into the team. Within one year, turnover was above 60%. Yes, more than half the team left.

To be fair to the leader, he was a competent guy who was stretched too thin. And that was *his* leaders' fault. But the overall point is this: As a leader, you set the tone for your team. This leader's casual, apathetic approach drove away serious people. They couldn't put their careers in the hands of this guy who thought reading Waffle House tweets was an acceptable way to spend an hour.

Key 4: Become a Learner

Here's the interesting part: This leader was a huge reader. He was smart, kept up with the latest ideas, and had a knowledgeable opinion on just about any topic. What if he'd brought some serious ideas to his team? Even if those ideas were unrelated to their specific line of work, even if they were a little random, what would that have communicated? It would have communicated that he took his team seriously, that he valued their time, and most importantly, that growth and learning mattered. A pointless meeting could have become a powerhouse of learning.

And learning is contagious. When you bring new ideas to your team, it creates excitement, challenges them to think differently, and helps them grow. You're showing your team what you value. You're raising the bar, and most of them will rise to meet it. Once you get them engaging with new ideas, they won't stop. And that's good for them, for you, and for your organization.

How to Become a Learner

You're currently reading or listening to this book, so you're already a learner. But I still want to offer a few simple and practical tips to help you make learning a lifelong priority.

Make Time

This point is going to be short and sweet: Make time in your schedule for learning. Every day. It has to be a priority.

You can maximize your time by learning while you do something else: commuting, exercising, eating lunch. Just make sure you can really focus on the learning. With exercise, for instance, cardio—with its steady pace—is probably better for learning than lifting weights. And maybe don't try to listen to an audiobook in a spin class.

But if you really want to get the most out of learning, I recommend setting aside time in the morning, which we'll talk about next.

Get Up Early

Jerry Seinfeld has a great bit about Night Guy vs. Morning Guy. Night guy always wants to stay up late, go out, have a good time. Getting up early? That's Morning Guy's problem. Here's what he says: "Night Guy always screws Morning Guy . . . The only thing Morning Guy can do is try and oversleep often enough so that Day Guy loses his job and Night Guy has no money to go out anymore."[4]

My advice? Get rid of Night Guy altogether—don't even give him a chance. Some of you won't like this one, but I'm going to say it anyway: Get up at 5 a.m. Be Morning Guy. It will change your life.

I told this to a buddy of mine a couple years ago. He said, "No way. I cannot do 5 a.m." I pestered him enough and he agreed to at least try it. He stuck with it, and his career's never been better.

I credit my ideas on this to Hal Elrod, author of *The Miracle Morning*. If you can't imagine waking up before the sun, read this book. Elrod gives you six things to do in the morning that are "guaranteed to save you from a life of unfulfilled potential."[5] I won't go into depth here on all of them. But one of those things is reading. For our purposes, that's the same thing as learning.

When you get up before everyone else, you have to time to breathe, to think, to process who you are and what you want to accomplish. This is a much more powerful way to learn than just listening to an audiobook while you ride the elliptical. (I don't want to discourage you from doing that— that's incredibly helpful too.) The benefit with waking up early is the silence. No one's emailing or calling yet. No one expects anything of you. You can sit with a book or podcast, take notes, and deeply process what you're learning.

If you have trouble waking up early, I suggest the 5 Second Rule developed by Mel Robbins. As soon as your alarm goes off, instead of hitting the snooze button, immediately start counting down from five: *5, 4, 3, 2, 1—Go.* The reason this works is because when you start counting, you're interrupting what researchers call "habit loops" that are encoded in your brain. You're also waking up your prefrontal cortex—the part of your brain that deals with executive functions and planning. Basically, you're tricking your brain. Robbins explains, "If you have an instinct to act on a

Key 4: Become a Learner

goal, you must physically move within five seconds or your brain will kill it."[6] The funny thing is, she discovered this by accident. As she kept using the technique and realized how well it worked, she started doing some research and found out that science backed it up.

So, feel free to try that the next time you're tempted to hit snooze. Waking up early not only gives you more time to learn, but also more time to write, which we'll talk about next.

Write

Several years ago, I started writing a blog called Marty's Minutes. My thought process went like this: I'm reading and learning all the time, and I want to share some of this with the world. But I don't think a book is the best place to start. Plus, who's going to read my book? No one's going to make that kind of time investment. But wouldn't they give me one minute? You'd give just about anybody a minute. And Marty's Minutes was born.

The interesting thing is, what really came out of it was my own growth. To be a learner wasn't just about reading. Writing became instrumental. It helped me understand all the information I was taking in. And this is when I started to be really successful—when I started writing down what I was learning to make sense of it. I was teaching myself by sharing ideas with the world.

That's why I believe writing has to be part of learning. Learning is usually passive, but writing makes it active. You wrestle with the ideas more when you have to explain them in your own words. *But Marty, I'm not a writer!* It doesn't matter. Not even a little. You're not doing this for anyone but yourself. Just start with five minutes a day. Make it part of the learning time that you'll schedule each day. Write a quick recap of what you've read or listened to. That's it.

Marty's Minutes got pretty popular at Advoco, so we started something called AMinutes. We challenged people at the company to be writers. They'd write a quick piece about a topic that interested them. They'd submit it, and the marketers would clean it up a bit and post it. So Marty's

Minutes turned into AMinutes and became a movement around the company.

Quick sidenote: How do you turn the people at your organization into learners? Make learning a core value. And not the kind of value you just give lip service to. You can tell a company's true core values by observing what they reward. If you truly want to know what a company values, ask them about the last promotion in their organization. What was it about that person that got them promoted? My guess is it wasn't one of the values written on the wall. If you value learning, promote it and reward it.

Okay, back to you and writing. Let's say you're ready to start writing. How do you know what to write about? It's simple: Start with what excites you.

Lean into What Excites You

As you start incorporating learning into your daily routine, you might wonder what you should be learning. How do you choose what book to read and podcast to listen to?

There's an old Buddhist quote that says, "When the student is ready the teacher will appear." When you start opening yourself up to learning, you'll find what you need. I think an easy way to figure out if you should dive into a certain book or podcast is to give it a try and see if it excites you. If it does, you're on the right path.

When I started Marty's Minutes, I was worried I wouldn't have enough topics to write about. But that was never an issue. Once I opened my eyes and looked for knowledge, I found a limitless supply.

When I was a salesman, I gravitated toward the greats, like Zig Ziglar. When I became a leader, what I needed to learn changed. So, I started engaging with people like Simon Sinek, Brené Brown, and Adam Grant.

There's no formula for this. The only real strategy here is to always maintain an open attitude toward learning. And don't learn out of a sense of obligation. You may not need to read the latest New York Times Best Seller. You may not need to subscribe to the trending podcast.

Key 4: Become a Learner

This isn't about keeping up with people. You're not learning to impress anyone or to win some game of mental gymnastics. You're learning to get better, to find things you can use in your real life.

Learning is about exploration and discovery. Trial and error. You'll stumble on amazing things as you start to search for the knowledge you need.

As fun as this process can be, learning isn't entertainment. You still need to challenge yourself. You might come across ideas that are difficult to grasp at first. If they're interesting to you, stick with them. But if you're reading a book and you keep falling asleep, maybe it's time to move on. Again, there's no formula. Be open and give things a chance. But if the spark isn't there, you don't need to force it. Pursue what excites you.

Develop a Growth Mindset

In Zen Buddhism, there's a concept known as *shoshin*, which means "beginner's mind." It's basically a state of mind that's open, humble, curious, and ready to learn. The idea with shoshin is that even if you're an expert in something, you're always looking to get better at it. And in a broader sense, you're willing to learn from everyone, everywhere, at any time.

The Avadhuta Gita, an ancient Hindu text, says, "One should never mind whether the teacher is a mere boy or one addicted to sensuous pleasures or whether he is an idiot or a menial servant or a householder. Would one give up a jewel lying in the mud?"

In other words, you can learn from almost anyone and almost any situation—as long as you're willing to keep an open mind.

For a modern, Western take on ideas like this, there's an amazing book called *Mindset: The New Psychology of Success* by Carol Dweck. She argues that people either have a *growth mindset* or a *fixed mindset*. People with a growth mindset believe they can learn just about anything. People with a fixed mindset believe they're either good at something or they're not. So basically, if they're not born with the ability, there's no point in trying. Guess who's more successful in life? Yep, people with growth mindsets.

Dweck is a professor at Stanford, so all of this is backed up with a ton of interesting research.

One of my favorite takeaways from the book has to do with the simple word *yet*. Take any situation where you feel in over your head, where everything's new or overwhelming, and use the "power of yet" to reframe it. For example, let's say you want to learn how to fly a plane. You sit in a cockpit for the first time, look at all the instruments and controls, and think, "I can't understand what any of this means . . . yet."

You can use yet for just about anything:

- "I can't do this . . . yet."
- "I'm not good at this . . . yet."
- "None of this makes sense . . . yet."

From learning computer code to installing a dishwasher to becoming a great leader, it's all intimidating at first. Of course you can't pull it off right away. People with a growth mindset seem to understand that there's nothing wrong with being a beginner. They know they'll make mistakes, and they're okay with that. They embrace challenges, learn from criticism, and push through setbacks. But the question is, why?

Because they truly believe that if they work hard enough, they can learn just about anything. They don't think that skills and abilities are set in stone. They believe in the power of yet and think, "I can't do this now, but I'll be able to if I put in the work."

Someone with a fixed mindset believes the opposite. As soon as they struggle with something, they think, *I'm not good at this*. And they quit. So, if they try to learn to play the guitar and the first few lessons are a struggle, they give up. They believe they don't have the ability, and there's no point in continuing on.

So, what if you've got a fixed mindset? That's okay. It's not set in stone. You can develop a growth mindset if you put in the work. And as a leader, you must have a growth mindset. Remember, all leaders are learners. You must believe you can learn any skill, develop any ability, and master any

Key 4: Become a Learner

field. Not because you're a once-in-a-generation genius, but because you're willing to put in the work.

In business and leadership, things change fast. It's easy to get overwhelmed and wonder if you'll be able to keep up. This is where a growth mindset is critical. Using the power of yet can help you stay hopeful and keep pushing: *I don't know how to adapt to this new technology . . . yet; I don't know how to get my business to the next level . . . yet; I can't figure out how to lead this younger generation . . . yet.*

As John Maxwell says, "Change is inevitable. Growth is optional." Choose a growth mindset. Don't put limits on yourself. You'll get the job done or find someone who can. You'll keep learning, keep pushing, and keep growing. That's what great leaders do.

Prime the Pump

One of my all-time favorite books is Zig Ziglar's *See You at the Top*. This was the first book that started to teach me the great game of business and leadership.

In his book, Ziglar tells the story of two of his friends who were driving in Alabama on a hot August day in the 1940s. They were thirsty, so they pulled up to a water pump behind an abandoned farmhouse. If you don't know what a water pump is, they were used to get clean water out of the ground. They were made of cast iron with a handle on top and a spout on the side where the water came out.

One of the men started pumping the handle, but nothing was coming out. After a while, he told his friend to grab a bucket and get some water from a nearby stream. He explained that in order to get the water flowing out, they'd first need to put some water in. This is referred to as *priming the pump*. At this point in the story, Ziglar says: "In the game of life, before you can get anything *out* you must put something in."[7]

Even after priming the pump, the man kept pumping the handle with no luck. His friend said, "I don't believe there's any water down there." His buddy, who was sweating by now, replied, "In south Alabama the wells are deep. And we're glad they're deep because the deeper the well the cooler, the cleaner, the sweeter, the purer, the better tasting the water is."[8]

Ziglar followed that up with, "And isn't that true in life?" He goes on to say that if you could become a medical doctor in six weeks of summer school, the reward for that would be next to nothing. And how many patients would come see you with that kind of education? We reward doctors with a high salary because they've put in twelve years of learning. They've pumped water from a deep well. It was difficult and time-consuming, but the water they drink is better because of it.

I love this story and the truth it illustrates. In fact, I was in Franklin, Tennessee, with my wife one day and I came across an old red water pump in an antique store. The price on it was seventy-five dollars. I picked it up, and my wife looked at me like I'd gone a little crazy. Well, I negotiated down to fifty dollars. Still probably too much, but I didn't care. My red water pump sits in my office and is a great reminder of a classic principle from Zig Ziglar.

As Ziglar says, "Anything worth doing is worth doing poorly until you can learn to do it well."[9] Being a lifelong learner is hard and it takes effort. And in most cases, you won't get the results right away. But if you invest your resources—whether that's time, energy, or money—and don't quit when things get difficult, there's no telling what you can accomplish. And the best part is, once that hard work is done, the water just flows. You don't need to work up a sweat to get a drink. With a quick movement of the handle, you'll have all the water you want.

Now, let's move on to the last key to becoming the leader people are happy to see: Be better.

Chapter 9

Key 5: Be Better

Back in the late '90s, the leaders at Chick-fil-A met to discuss how they were going to compete with a fast-growing restaurant that was popping up everywhere, Boston Market. They gathered around their visionary leader, Truett Cathy, looking for guidance and a plan for how they could beat this new competitor that had set a terrifying goal: Boston Market planned to hit $1 billion in sales by the year 2000.

Picture Truett, with his warm Southern charm, sitting quietly as the leaders at his up-and-coming fast-food chain discussed how to get bigger, faster. Truett hadn't said anything for a long time, then out of nowhere, he pounded his fist on the table until the room got quiet. And he delivered a message that wasn't just a pep talk but a profound philosophy. "Gentlemen, I am sick and tired of hearing you talk about us getting bigger. If we get just *get better*, our customers will demand that we get bigger."[1]

With that one sentence, Truett ignited a cultural mindset that would fuel the success of one of America's most successful fast-food chains. In 2000, Chick-fil-A hit $1 billion in sales, and Boston Market filed for bankruptcy.

Truett was talking about more than just business strategy. His words were a call to a higher standard in every area of the company, including personal growth. He believed that by pouring their hearts into making each day better than the last, the rest would take care of itself. It wasn't a battle against competitors; it was a quest for self-improvement.

That moment in the boardroom became a brushstroke, illustrating the ethos of continuous improvement and customer devotion that still defines

Key 5: Be Better

Chik-fil-A today. With one sentence, Truett summed up a whole philosophy: If you focus on getting better, the world will demand more of your greatness.

This idea inspired the fifth key to becoming the leader people are happy to see: Be better. Don't let the simplicity of it fool you. This key focuses your energy and attention in a powerful way.

As leaders we spend so much time worrying about things we cannot control. Just like we cannot control the weather, we cannot control our competition. We cannot control the economy, and we certainly cannot control how our customers are going to act.

What we can control is how we think. In the middle of all the uncertainty, we can repeat the mantra, "Just be better every day." That's a message of hope—a message that says we can control ourselves and our actions. If we just focus on becoming a better version of ourselves, then how can we go wrong?

The Infinite Game

In his book *The Infinite Game,* Simon Sinek delves into the concept of game theory and how it relates to business. In game theory, there are two types of mindsets: finite and infinite. A finite mindset focuses on winning and competition. They see themselves as playing a game that has an ending, fixed rules, and a clear winner. Basically, they think business is a game like baseball or poker. This leads them to take actions that get quick results because they view success as a finite resource that everyone's competing for. They prioritize immediate gains at the expense of future opportunities and stability. In business, this mindset can lead to a culture that measures success in terms of victories and losses rather than progress and development.

Someone with an infinite mindset, on the other hand, realizes that the game they're playing doesn't have fixed rules, and it never ends. You don't win or lose the game, you just eventually stop playing, and the game goes on without you. Politics, business, life itself—these are all examples of infinite games.

FINDING SIGNIFICANCE

Leaders and organizations with an infinite mindset prioritize resilience, adaptability, and visionary thinking. They focus on their values and think long term. They see their "competitors" not as rivals to be beaten, but as players in the same game that continues indefinitely. This perspective is important because it encourages collaboration, innovation, and a commitment to a cause or purpose that goes beyond mere financial gain or market dominance. The aim is to build a lasting and evolving legacy rather than to secure immediate victories. Simply put, in the infinite game there are no winners or losers, just people participating. No one can win the game because the game never ends.

When we think about this concept, it changes everything about the way we lead and the way we view our roles. Truett Cathy understood the infinite game. Chik-fil-A was not in competition with other restaurants—they were in competition with themselves. If they just got better, customers would demand they get bigger. And we all know how this has turned out for them.

Moving to an infinite mindset and focusing on just being better was a turning point in our company's evolution. When we stopped worrying about what other people were doing and just focused on us and how we could better serve our customers, our numbers soared.

Take a minute to think back to those five words you wrote when you answered the question, "What do I want my leadership brand to be?" Do your words line up with a finite or an infinite mindset? If some of them lean toward a finite mindset, then change them. In today's complex business environment, it's crucial to recognize that you're playing an infinite game. It's not about winning a specific contest—it's about adapting and growing so you can become the best player possible.

Dabo Swinney and the Three-Legged Stool

In 2018, one of my best friends gave me a special gift. He invited me to join him and a few other guys to meet Dabo Swinney, the head football coach at Clemson University. Now, if you don't know Dabo, he's a legend. He's the winningest coach in Clemson history. The team has won two

Key 5: Be Better

national championships under his leadership, and lots of people consider his 2018 championship team to be the greatest team in the history of college football.

And this was the team I got to meet. This was spring 2018, so they hadn't won the championship yet, and they were still a few months from starting the season. But this team was impressive and stacked with future NFL players: Trevor Lawrence, Christian Wilkins, Dexter Lawrence, Hunter Renfrow, Tee Higgins, and many other superstars.

Before we met Dabo, we took a tour of Clemson's athletic facilities. Everything was amazing—from where they displayed their trophies to the players cafeteria. It was all top-notch.

Then we made our way to Dabo's office. On the way there, my wheels were turning. When you meet someone like him, you don't just want to ask questions about football. You want to think of something really unique or interesting—something he hasn't answered a thousand times.

When we got to his office, I saw a three-legged stool off to the side. It was small—you'd have to squat down to sit on its little leather seat. When I asked Dabo about it, his eyes lit up. He told us that this stool was a gift from one of his friends. His buddy went on a trip to Puerto Rico, visited a remote fishing village, and brought back one of these stools for Dabo. In that village, the men would sit around on these stools at the end of the day and talk about fishing and family and life.

Around the time Dabo was gifted this stool, he was struggling to figure out why his team didn't make it to the national championship game the previous season. It was the most talented team he'd ever coached. They should've been contenders for the title. Dabo had a hunch that the team just wasn't connected enough. Football teams are huge—120 players or more, plus a big coaching and training staff. It's not easy to get that many young men from all walks of life to bond with each other. That's when Dabo had an idea.

After practice one day, he put the fishing stool in the middle of the team meeting room. All the guys are standing around and there's this tiny stool next to Dabo. He tells the guys this stool is a "safe seat"—it's a place to share, to be yourself, and to be vulnerable. Then he invites one of the players to sit in the stool, and he asks him questions about his life—where he came from, what life was like growing up, what kind of hardships he faced, what were his defining moments. Then Dabo lets the team ask questions too.

Dabo did this after every practice. Every single player—even three-hundred-pound, six foot five Dexter Lawrence—sat down on the tiny stool and got vulnerable. The team learned so much about each other. Some guys were brought to tears.

Sitting in that little stool broke down walls—ego and pride came crumbling down. The team bonded. They connected in an authentic way.

Some people think it's weak to do that kind of thing—sharing and getting real. But it made the team stronger than ever. They won the championship that year. And they probably shouldn't have. On paper, they weren't as talented as the team from the previous season. But Dabo believes that the "safe seat" made the difference. It became a major part of their winning formula.

It wasn't strategy or talent or intense training that made this team into champions. It was connection. Authentic bonds. Dabo was playing the infinite game. He knew that setting aside time to connect would make these guys better. And not just better players—better people.

Not long after Dabo finished telling us about the stool, someone came to tell him it was time for practice. We followed him out and got to watch all the drills and plays from the sidelines, which was awesome. We were just a few feet away from quarterback Trevor Lawrence, who would go on to be the number one draft pick in a few years.

After practice, everyone gathered around Dabo, and we were allowed to join the huge huddle. All 120 guys were standing there. And it was completely silent. For me, this became the highlight of the day. Everything else was great, but this talk that Dabo dropped on these young men was phenomenal. I'll never forget what I heard.

Key 5: Be Better

Remember, this would be their last practice for a couple months. So Dabo was wrapping up the season. He started by thanking them for their hard work. Then he went on for forty-five minutes while these guys—big guys—quietly stood there, hanging on every word.

Dabo told them how important they are to the community and the people around them. That what he wants from them is not awards and accolades, but for each of them to become the best version of themselves that they can be.

He then told all of them to schedule time on his calendar with his secretary. He wanted to talk with each one of them about what they wanted in life, where they wanted to be, and how he could help them get there. And he didn't mean that in terms of football. He said that only a few of them could be All-Americans or superstars. That's the reality of the game they're a part of. He told them that the biggest challenge they will face won't come on the football field—it'll come from the struggle to be better versions of themselves.

What Dabo was trying to get through to these guys was that football is a finite game. It ruthlessly picks winners and losers, and it eventually ends. For most of the players, that ending would come sooner than later. He wanted them to start thinking beyond football—about who they are as people, about the qualities they could develop that would help them no matter where life took them. He wanted them to play the infinite game and focus on being better.

Be Better Attitudes

The common thread so far in this chapter is that you've got three guys—Truett Cathey, Simon Sinek, and Dabo Swinney—from very different backgrounds and industries reaching the same conclusion: Success isn't about beating anyone or winning anything specific, it's about focusing on making yourself better.

And let's not forget who these guys are. Dabo Swinney is a master at winning in the finite game of football. Truett Cathey dominated as a newcomer in the competitive fast-food industry. And Simon Sinek is a best-selling business author.

I don't know about you, but I didn't expect these "be better" ideas to come from a football coach, a titan in the fast-food industry, and a business expert. All three of these men are in industries where success is mostly viewed in terms of winners and losers. But they all won their respective finite games by continually focusing on the infinite game.

And they're all saying the same thing—handing us the secret to success in life, business, and leadership: Focus on being better.

After that day I spent with Dabo and his team, I started thinking about the EntreLeadership conference I'd attended a couple years before. If you remember the story, that conference was a turning point for me, my career, and my company. And that's where the idea of intentionality made a huge impact on me. But something else had been rolling around in my head since that conference—something that I came to call the "Be Better Attitudes."

These are a set of attitudes that can change not only your thoughts and actions, but also those of your team and organization. What I learned is the only thing stopping me and my team from being great was ourselves.

Here are the ten Be Better Attitudes:

1. Be Present
2. Be Inclusive
3. Be Courageous
4. Be Excellent
5. Be Driven
6. Be Knowledgeable
7. Be Accountable
8. Be Innovative
9. Be Trustworthy
10. Be Better

We'll unpack each of these below. But first I want to say a little more about these attitudes.

Key 5: Be Better

I've mentioned this before but it's worth repeating: A key to success is to stop focusing on specific, long-term goals and start focusing on direction. In life, you'll run into failure and you'll run into success. You can't often predict when or how either will happen, but what you can do is control how you'll behave no matter what comes your way. And that increases your odds of succeeding over time.

The first part of focusing on direction is figuring out what you value and who you'd like to be. This is what you did back in chapter 2. You wrote down the words you'd like people to use to describe your leadership brand. You were stating what you value. And you were setting a direction—you'll work toward becoming that kind of leader. You'll still set goals along the way—goals aren't a bad thing—but what truly guides you is the destination you've chosen. You're looking down the road and thinking about who you want to be and what you want people to remember you for.

When you don't set a direction, you can easily end up caught in what author Sean Covey calls the "whirlwind," which we talked about in chapter 3: "The *whirlwind* of urgent activity required to keep things running day-to-day which devoured all the time and energy…needed to execute the strategy *for* tomorrow."[2]

And that's where the Be Better Attitudes come in. They keep you intentional. They take you from *wanting* to be a great leader to *acting* like a great leader. When you focus on them, how can you fail? They force you to address the very needs that are missing in most businesses and leaders. When you incorporate them into your life, they set you on the right path. I know this firsthand—for so many years, I let the whirlwind choose my path. And that kept me from being the leader I could've been.

Daniel Coyle, in the *The Culture Code: The Secrets of Highly Successful Groups* said, "While successful culture can look and feel like magic, the truth is that it's not. Culture is a set of living relationships working toward a shared goal. It's not something you are. It's something you do." Just like successful cultures, great leaders are only great because of what they *do*. Aspirations, hopes, dreams—they don't get the job done. They're an important starting point, but great leadership is a result of doing the right things *every day*.

Keep that in mind as you go through the list of Be Better Attitudes. You want to adopt these attitudes so they can guide your actions.

You might notice that there's nothing on this list that hasn't been written about before or that's revolutionary. But taken together as a whole, these attitudes become an operating system for you, and hopefully for your team and organization as well. When you address all the areas we'll discuss, you will become the leader, I think, most of us want to be.

1. Be Present

As leaders, we're future-oriented. We're all about the next quarter, the next goal, the next meeting. Is this a bad thing? No—part of your present responsibility is thinking about the future. But being future-oriented goes bad when it overtakes the present all the time. Here's what this looks like: You're in one meeting thinking about the next one. You're talking to someone while thinking about your next call. You're with your family worrying about sales revenue. No one gets all your attention. You're never where you are. Some part of you is always drifting into the future.

This leads to anxiety and stress. And ultimately, fear. It may not be a conscious sense of fear, but it's there. You're afraid if you don't worry about it right now, it won't get done. Or it won't get done properly.

The first casualty of fear is your leadership brand. Fear makes you forget who you are, what you value, and where you want to go. Fear makes you reactive, not intentional. You're short with your kids, you lash out at your team—you create lots of moments, just not the kind you'd want anyone to remember.

So, how do you stay present? One thing you can do is block time on your schedule to think about the future. Once that time block is over, you're back in the present.

And the second way is to remember who you want to be. When you wrote down those words about your leadership brand, that wasn't a one-and-done thing. Those words need to be part of your daily life. Put them on your bathroom mirror, on your car's dashboard, wherever you'll see them a lot. Stay conscious of who you want to be and the legacy you want to create.

You're building a leadership brand, and you do that *now*. In the moment. Every day. With every interaction. If you get that right, the future will take care of itself.

2. Be Inclusive

If your first thought is DEI (diversity, equity, and inclusion), that's not what I mean here. It's more than that. Hiring people from different backgrounds, ethnicities, and age groups is a good thing. But bringing them on board doesn't mean you're actually including them. Being inclusive means you listen to them.

I brought a buddy of mine to the Advoco office one day. I introduced him to some engineering interns, and he asked them if they liked working there. "Man, we love it!" My buddy was taken aback: "Love it? *Love* is a big word. What'd you love about it?"

"They trust us. They give us tough problems to solve. Every day is fun because it's a challenge."

That's being inclusive. These interns were at the bottom of the totem pole, but they felt like they mattered. And they *did* matter. We gave them real work and took their problem-solving seriously.

Being inclusive is trusting people to do their jobs. It's listening to their ideas no matter who they are. You hired them, so if you trust your hiring process, you need to trust your people.

One more thought here: Truly successful people got where they are by surrounding themselves with talented individuals. Race, age, religion—none of it matters to them. But the trap a lot of companies fall into is letting a lot of different kinds of people through their doors and then never hearing from them again.

Listen to your team. Listen to their ideas. You need all those diverse perspectives and opinions. It will make your company stronger.

3. Be Courageous

Being courageous is one of my core principles. You have to be willing to take risks and make mistakes. This doesn't mean you get a pass for lazy decision-making. Learn to analyze situations, gather necessary information, and make timely decisions. Then own them. There's always a risk you'll get it wrong, and that's where courage comes in.

Now, here's where next-level courage comes in: Extend that same courtesy and grace to your team. Give them the chance to make the wrong decision. Let them mess up. That's how they learn to take ownership and become better people.

I think a lot of leaders fear giving their team this kind of freedom—and not for the reasons you'd think. You'd assume it's because they're afraid the team will fail. And that's certainly part of it, particularly for leaders who struggle with trust. But the real fear? That the team will succeed.

Here's the thought process: *If my team makes its own decisions and can operate successfully without my input, then I'm not necessary.* That fear causes a lot of leaders to rein their teams in. But it's courageous to let them go and let them succeed. If they can run the place without you, then you've done your job. And the truth is, the more successful they are, the more you'll be needed. A successful, empowered team is a happy, fulfilled team. And that kind of team creates growth. That means you'll have plenty to do.

And there's a larger principle operating here that's more important than the assurance you'll still be needed: The more you give, the more you'll receive. If you allow your team to shine, guide them toward success, and invest in their growth, it'll all come back to you.

In the end, we won't be measured by our sales numbers, wins and losses, or the size of the company we built—we will be measured by the difference we made in people's lives. So be courageous and help your people become the best they can be.

4. Be Excellent

I needed some carpentry work done on my house recently, and I got in touch with a carpenter named Garrett. This guy impressed the hell out of

Key 5: Be Better

me. You know why? He showed up when he said he'd show up. Every time.

I passed his name on to my neighbors—who are very picky when it comes to their house—and they loved him. I'm sure you can guess why. He showed up on time. They didn't mention his amazing carpentry skills (though they're really good). They didn't mention his prices or how fast he worked. They were in awe that this guy said he'd be there at 9 a.m. and was there at 9 a.m.

If you've ever gotten some significant work done on your house, you're probably wishing you had Garrett's number right now. In the contracting world, being late is almost a given. Garrett is outperforming 95% of his competition by just doing what he says he's going to do.

And that's one huge part of excellence: doing what you say you'll do. Following through. Showing up. So many people flake out on the basics that being a dependable human being has become a wow factor.

I'm going to let you in on a secret: It's not hard to be great. The bar is so low.

Now, hopefully you don't read that and think, *Nice. I can get by half-assing it*. What you should be thinking is, *That means there's a lot of opportunity for me to shine*. You can either be another face in the crowd or you can be someone who stands out. Excellence makes you stand out.

What does excellence look like as a leader? Let me give you six behaviors.

First, it's what I've already mentioned. Do what you say you'll do. Be on time. Follow through. Be dependable. And do that for everyone—your leaders, your clients, and those you lead.

Second, develop the "excellence reflex." This idea comes from Danny Meyer's book *Setting the Table*. If you don't know who Meyer is, he built a restaurant empire in New York City and started the burger chain Shake Shack. Here's what he says: "People duck as a natural reflex when something is hurled at them. Similarly, the excellence reflex is a natural reaction to fix something that isn't right, or to improve something that could be better. The excellence reflex is rooted in instinct…and then constantly honed through awareness, caring, and practice."[3] If someone throws a plate at your head, you react. You don't think. You just duck or dodge. Meyer says that's exactly what you should do when something is subpar in business. Just start fixing it.

This brings us to the third way to be excellent: Stop blaming, start solving. I can't tell you how many times I've seen a team get hung up on finding out who to blame. A problem pops up and they don't look for a solution—they look for someone to blame. As a leader, nip this in the bud. Solve the issue—that's the priority. If you need to figure out who to blame for a specific reason, do it after the problem is solved. But in a lot of cases, it just doesn't matter.

Fourth, do the right thing. You usually know exactly what the right thing is. Do it when it's tough. Do it when it hurts. Provide excellent service for your customers and do the right thing when you mess up. Same goes for your team.

Fifth, do common things in an uncommon way. In other words, focus on the little things. The path to excellence is paved with attention to detail. If we focus on small, consistent, intentional actions, we will achieve extraordinary things. Here's why: The way we do the little things is the way we do the big things. Excellence is created by many thousands of small decisions that create actions that create results.

Lastly, say no. Part of being excellent is knowing when to say no. Remember Garrett the carpenter? If he started saying yes to too many jobs, he'd stop showing up on time. That's a good way to ruin his brand. Say no to the meeting if you know you can't prepare properly. Say no to the project if you know you can't give it your best. Don't overcommit. Understand your limits. Excellence is showing up fully.

One final thought: Excellence is not perfection. It's being the best you can possibly be, but that will never be perfect. So don't let the quest for excellence stop you from taking action. That's being a perfectionist. Just do your best. That's all you can do.

5. Be Driven

I can sum this one up in three words: Get shit done.

Don't get this confused with staying busy. It's not about the number of meetings you go to or the long hours you work. It's about the results you get. Work and results are two very different things. You can work a ton and get no results. And you can work a little and get big results.

That's why it's so important to start any project or endeavor by understanding what success looks like. When you know what winning looks like, you can efficiently manage your time and focus on high-priority activities that will yield results.

Can you control the results you get? No, not often. But that's why you should be intentional about how you spend your time. You want to focus on the tasks that are most likely to move the needle.

I need to add a really important point here: Teach your team to have this mindset too. And give them the freedom to operate this way.

As a leader, having a results mindset means you have to stop getting distracted by minor factors. Maybe a salesman wants to work from 5 a.m. to noon and spend afternoons with his family. Is he getting results? Great, let him do it. Why are we hung up on what I like to call "work theater"? So many people are pretending to be busy—they're just running out the clock, waiting for the 5 p.m. bell to ring. Anyone can sit in a chair for eight hours. I'd rather have someone there for half that time if they can get shit done.

You're a responsible adult, so treat your team like responsible adults. This is how I look at it: I'm not in the business of micromanaging time or grading effort. I do not play the "work theater" game. I trust that my team cares about the results that drive the team forward, that they care about their own lives and careers, and that they will manage their time in the best way for them.

You know what would get my attention? If they stopped getting results. But if they leave at 3 p.m. on Tuesday to get their oil changed, I don't really care.

FINDING SIGNIFICANCE

My friend works for an accounting firm. During the busy season, the expectation was that they'd work seven days a week. It's a thing in the accounting world—you have to go hard. It's just what everyone does.

But my friend told me, they didn't actually work that hard. Everyone knew they'd be there Saturday and Sunday, so they just sort of coasted during the week. They could've gotten a lot more done and enjoyed their weekends at home. But they had to keep up the appearance of working hard by coming in on Saturday and Sunday. It would have been unthinkable not to. So they played the game. How ridiculous is that?

It reminds me of the movie *Office Space*. Here's what the main character tells a couple consultants who are trying to figure out how everyone at the company spends their time: "Well, I generally come in at least fifteen minutes late…after that, I sort of space out for about an hour…I just stare at my desk. But it looks like I'm working. I do that for probably another hour after lunch too. I'd say in a given week I probably only do about fifteen minutes of real actual work."[4]

This is why everyone on your team should have a PSF (see chapter 6). What does success look like for them? How do you know if they're getting results? For the sales and marketing teams, it's easy to see. But it can be tough for other teams. You might have people coasting along and only putting in fifteen minutes a week—but they look really busy. Or—and what I think is more likely—you've got all-stars who are crushing it, and you don't even know.

Don't be fooled by busyness—in your own life or on your team. Be driven to get results, and be equipped to measure results.

6. Be Knowledgeable

Right before I started writing this section, I saw a post from Chris Voss on my Instagram feed. If you don't know Voss, he's a former FBI hostage negotiator who wrote *Never Split the Difference*. His post was genius. I won't get into the details, but it was an excellent piece of negotiation training. Well, I read that and went down a rabbit hole, reading and watching more and more of Voss's material.

I mention that because it's a perfect example of how to be knowledgeable. I had some extra time, and I learned something new. That's really how simple this is. I could've watched funny reels or checked the news, but I made the choice to expose myself to something that had the potential to make me better. It sounds like I'm patting myself on the back here, but what I'm really trying to get across is that gaining knowledge doesn't have to be complicated.

I don't need to spend much time on this topic because we already hit on it pretty hard in Key 4: Become a Learner. So I'll just sum this up with three quick ideas:

- You're not that smart (neither am I), so you better keep learning new things to give yourself an edge.
- What got you here isn't going to get you there. You'll need a new knowledge base to get to the next level.
- Your mindset matters. Embrace a growth mindset that continuously seeks knowledge and improvement, particularly when it comes to trends in your industry.

7. Be Accountable

As a leader, it's on you to hold yourself *and* your team accountable. And you do that in two distinct areas: results and behaviors.

I talked a lot about the importance of results in the Be Driven section. Results make it easy to hold someone accountable because they're measurable. Once you've set expectations, you just see if the person measures up. And this is something you must do. You might hire the nicest, smartest person in the world, but if they're not getting results, something has to change. But results are only one side of the coin. To hold you and your team accountable, you must evaluate results *and* behaviors.

Let's say you've got an all-star salesperson on your team. Maybe you took my advice in the Be Driven section and eased up on policing your team on the minor stuff. So, this guy's not at his desk for half the day. That's fine, right? Sure, as long as it doesn't affect his results. But then he starts showing up late to mandatory meetings. And he hasn't filled out expense reports for a couple months. He's getting results, so nothing else matters, right? Wrong. You shouldn't be a micromanager, but you still need to be a regular manager. You have to hold him accountable for results *and* behavior.

Here's why: The rest of the team is watching. If you don't rein this guy in, three things happen next: (1) Morale plummets because the team sees there's one set of rules for them and another for this salesman; (2) Some of them start testing the waters and seeing what they can get away with; and (3) Mr. All-Star's ego inflates, and he will eventually cross lines that hurt your whole company.

By the way, all of this applies to you as well. You don't get a pass for being an asshole because you're crushing it on the results end. Good performance doesn't excuse bad behavior.

And when things *aren't* going well—revenue drops, turnover is high, campaigns fail—don't look for someone else to blame. Own it. Take responsibility. It's your job to change course and make it better.

And when profits are up and everything's awesome, don't take the credit. Shine the spotlight on your team. The worst behaviors of a bad leader are blaming other people when things go wrong and taking all the credit when things go right.

Own the failures and pass on the successes. It's tough, but it's what great leaders do.

Let's see how being accountable plays out with a real-world example. At Advoco, we helped companies install complex manufacturing software and systems. For instance, we worked with one of the world's largest soft drink companies. Imagine how complex one of their bottling plants is and what it takes to keep it running 24/7. When we'd install one of these systems, we'd lay out the required maintenance. This was necessary, preventative stuff to keep everything running smoothly. But what we often encountered were mechanics who would just say, "Yeah, I'm not doing any of that. It's not my job." And believe it or not, they'd get away with it.

Key 5: Be Better

Now, these weren't our employees. They were our clients' employees, so there wasn't much we could do about it, even though we knew it wasn't going to end well if they didn't do the necessary tasks. But these mechanics and maintenance guys were irritated about the new system. They didn't want to learn anything new or do anything different.

What's going on here is a lack of accountability. A behavior problem is going to lead to a results problem. The plant is going to run better than ever—for a while. Eventually the lack of maintenance will hurt productivity and revenue.

How does this get solved? First, in the hiring process. Never hire anyone who has an "it's not my job" mentality. Look for people who have the "excellence reflex," which we already talked about. Second, get maintenance tasks written into all current and future mechanics' PSFs. Then you can hold them accountable for results. Basically, *make it* their job. And finally, the behavior problem. For some reason, these mechanics feel like they can do whatever they want. That's a leadership and culture failure.

The leaders at these plants upgraded to expensive, state-of-the-art systems that would get better results. In that way, they were being proactive and holding themselves accountable. But they weren't holding the teams below them accountable. Sure, they were probably five steps removed from the mechanic who refused to do his job, but it was still on them to make sure the proper maintenance was happening. And when the plant runs into problems—and it inevitably will—it'll be on them to own it. Either that, or they can find someone else to blame.

Do you see how important accountability is? A couple mechanics with bad attitudes can ruin a massive capital investment. When bad results and bad behaviors pop up—yours or your team's—deal with them *fast*. When you let them linger, you're sanctioning incompetence. And that can quickly spread through your team and organization.

8. Be Innovative

You know the British company Dyson? You've probably seen their bagless vacuums or bladeless fans or used their hand dryers in public restrooms. They're constantly reimagining and improving products that we all take for granted. Their mission statement—"Solve the problems others seem to ignore"—is a motto any businessperson or leader should live by.

James Dyson, who founded the company and invented the world's first bagless vacuum, said this about his approach to business: "If you always do what you know is going to work, you'll have less failure. But you'll never make a substantive change or a breakthrough….What we're trying to do is something different and better….We're risk-taking all the time. We're stepping off into the unknown….And we've gathered round us a group of people who want to do that."[5]

Throughout my career, I've continually learned new things. I'm old enough to remember when the Internet was brand-new! And you know what? I immediately learned about "this thing called the Internet." I've tried to stay ahead of the curve by learning marketing, negotiation, sales management, CRMs. While others said, "It's not my job. I don't have time for that," I took it on. There's a term for that called *talent stacking*. You make yourself more valuable and more interesting by adding to your tool belt, by bringing more to the table.

On of our HR guys at Advoco did this. When we started using the Working Genius and the DISC tests, he dug in. He became an expert at them. Then he just kept adding to his tool belt. Eventually he became VP of Operations because he'd managed to make himself very valuable and a lot more interesting.

You've got to be adaptable in the face of change. The business landscape is dynamic, and being able to adapt is crucial for long-term success. Be curious. When you don't know something, find out. Ask why. A curious mindset means you're open to shifting your beliefs and strategies. Find new solutions, and explore the unknown. Truly good leaders are always looking for new ways to do things.

Key 5: Be Better

For Dyson, it hasn't always worked out. They've got a ton of failed products, most notably an electric car project that they abandoned after pouring $500 million into it. But their spirit of innovation and their ability to think differently has led to amazing success.

One last thought here: A lot has been said about leaders surrounding themselves with smart people. I agree with this, but maybe not for the usual reasons. Many leaders think they should do this so they can sit back and let the talent do all the hard work and innovating—as if the leader is a pro sports general manager. Put the right team together and let the wins roll in. But that's not the right approach. You need to think of yourself more as a player-coach. You should be playing the game right alongside your team. You should be learning and innovating as much as or more than them. The reason you should surround yourself with smart people is so you can get smarter.

9. Be Trustworthy

Trust is the cornerstone of everything we do as leaders. Your reputation, your business, your leadership brand—it all rests on trust. And if you lose trust, it all comes crashing down.

Trust starts with being open and honest with yourself. You have to face the reality of who you really are and what your blind spots might be. We talked a lot about this in chapter 4, Controlling Your Ego, so I won't dig in on it here. But I can sum it up simply: If you're bullshitting yourself, it's way easier to bullshit other people. So tell yourself the truth. Then you'll have the right foundation to build trust as a leader.

You build trust with your team by consistently demonstrating honesty and ethical behavior. In other words, lead with integrity. It's never wrong to do what's right. That applies to your interactions with customers and colleagues too. Don't lie. Don't stretch the numbers or research to fit your narrative. Don't cover up bad behavior. This is the stuff you learned in kindergarten or Sunday School, and it still matters.

Trust isn't like a bank account. You can't put a bunch of trust in, then withdraw a little bit, and still have a lot of trust left over. You wipe out all of it with one bad move. You make one withdrawal from that trust account and your balance is zero.

A lack of trust is why people leave companies. They don't trust leadership to do the right thing. And here's the interesting part about trust: It's more than just telling the truth or following rules. People need to feel like they're in good hands—like you want something *for* them, not always something *from* them. You build this kind of trust by doing a lot of the things we've talked about in this book already—caring about your team as individuals, investing in them, and listening to their ideas.

In one of his last interviews before he passed away, Steve Jobs said, "If you want to hire great people and have them stay working for you, you have to let them make a lot of decisions and you have to be run by ideas, not hierarchy. The best ideas have to win, otherwise good people don't stay."[6] At its core, this is a quote about trust. People want to know that their opinions are valued, that leadership will listen, that their voice matters. That's how they know they're in good hands, and that's also how they know they have agency over their career. They know that if they put in the effort to come up with creative ideas, they'll be heard.

This is just one example of how you can build trust into your culture. And this kind of trust goes beyond ethics and honesty. Overall, you want a culture where people feel respected. And that starts with what you do, not just what you say. Core values, slogans on the walls, speeches in staff meetings—those are empty words if they're not backed up by actions. In the end, you can't prove trust. You can't point to stats that show you deserve it. It's a feeling. Your team will decide whether you're trustworthy based on how you're making them feel in everyday interactions.

Maybe you're reading this and thinking about how you've lost your team's trust. How do you rebuild it? The first thing you should do is admit to them where you went wrong. After that, you put in the long, slow work of rebuilding. It'll take time. But when they see that you're not repeating your mistakes, they'll eventually trust you again. The same goes if you've lost trust with customers or colleagues.

Key 5: Be Better

Trust is a fragile thing. Warren Buffet said, "It takes 20 years to build a reputation and five minutes to ruin it."[7] Fortunately, even if you feel like you've blown it or you haven't been great at building trust, you can make it right. Stephen Covey said, "Contrary to what most people believe, trust is not some soft, illusive quality that you either have or you don't; rather, trust is a pragmatic, tangible, actionable asset that you can *create*."[8]

In business, we think we're dealing with money, but every purchase, deal, or contract starts and ends with trust. In fact, the only real currency you have in life is trust. It's a precious commodity. Don't squander it.

10. Be Better

I know I'm probably breaking some kind of rule here by having "Be Better" as part of my "Be Better Attitudes." I get it. I don't care, but I get it. I'm passionate about this topic—we need better leaders. In every industry. Every company. In government. In nonprofits. In families. In schools. And I'm talking about leaders who are better in any and every way. They're hungry, curious, driven, and overflowing with integrity. We've got enough assholes in charge—let's be better!

Listen, I'm sixty-three years old, and I have never been more excited in my life than now to get better and learn more. Growth doesn't have to stop. It's a mindset and a choice. No matter who you are or where you're at in life, you can be better than you were yesterday.

I know a lot of leaders, and so many of them have stopped growing. They hit a certain point and that's it. In a lot of cases, it's because they feel like they've arrived. They got their C-suite title by doing x, y, z, so they just keep doing x, y, z. In other cases, they want to keep moving up, but they don't want to stretch themselves anymore. They've let that muscle atrophy—and it's tough for them to adapt to new ideas and ways of looking at themselves and the world.

Don't let that happen to you. Keep striving to be better.

When you get better, your team will get better, and your company culture will get better. And that makes the world a little bit better.

I don't know where you're at in the company hierarchy, but the higher up you are, the more influence you have to make the company culture better. And it won't get better through parties or events. Too many companies think that's what culture is. None of that stuff makes up for a negative environment or employees dealing with a lack of respect all day. The fanciest, most high-end party in the world doesn't change how people feel about their company on a day-to-day level. If you want a happy team, be the leader who pushes themselves and their team to live by these Be Better Attitudes.

The last thing I want to say here might seem a little out of left field, but I think it's important: Have some fun. When I see a struggling leader, I'm usually looking at someone who takes themselves too seriously. Part of being better is realizing you're not that important. Lighten up and enjoy the journey.

We only have one life. Work will always be part of it for most of us. We should enjoy our time at work just as much as time outside of it. And that can happen when you create a respectful environment where people feel valued. When that's the foundation, it's easy to have fun with the people you're building your company with.

At my former company, my partners and I were the last ones to leave any of our events. We didn't force ourselves to do that. We loved to be there. This was a big difference from what I'd seen at other companies. Normally the top leaders would make an appearance, make a few rounds, and duck out early. What's that communicating to their team? That they don't want to be there. Then why would their team want to be there? And why wouldn't these leaders want to be around the awesome people who are helping them make a nice living and grow their company?

What I'm getting at is this: Enjoy your team. Don't take them for granted. If you have some influence, use it to make your company a place where you enjoy spending your time. That starts with lots of mutual respect and should end with lots of fun.

Just be better.

Part III

What Causes Good People to Become Bad Leaders?

Chapter 10

You Might Be a Bad Leader If . . .

I have to admit something. *Finding Significance* was not the original title of this book. My first working title was *You Don't Have to Be an Asshole to Be a Leader*. I changed it for a few reasons.

First, my wife wasn't thrilled with it, and she made some good arguments for a new title. Did I want to be the "asshole" guy?

Second, this book is about more than just avoiding bad behaviors. It's about implementing positive changes and finding deeper purpose and significance as a leader. In other words, it's not just about what to avoid, but about what to *become*.

Lastly, a friend read a rough draft and wanted to recommend it to a colleague. But he told me he felt like he'd be calling her an asshole if he did. I didn't want my book to have that negative vibe.

The funny thing is, almost everyone loved the original title. Whenever I said I was going to change it, they'd say, "No, don't—it's perfect!" And then they'd get that smirk on their face. Everyone has worked for an asshole.

Before I switched the title to *Finding Significance*, I took a writing class from Donald Miller in Nashville. On the way to an event, my Uber driver asked me why I was in town. I told him I was writing a book, and I was here to learn more about the process. Well, naturally, the next question out of his mouth was, "That's exciting—what's your book about?"

"It's called *You Don't Have to Be an Asshole to Be a Leader*," I said.

You should have seen his reaction. He jumped all over it telling me story after story about the bosses he'd had and what jerks they were. The more he told the stories the more I could see the frustration just boiling over. Then he said, "Why do they have to be that way, I'm just trying to do my job."

Every time I meet with a company, I ask people to raise their hand if they've ever worked for an asshole. Everyone's hands shoot up. Unfortunately, assholes are everywhere, and no matter how much training goes on, we seem to produce more every day.

So, I keep asking myself, *What causes good people to become really bad leaders?*

What causes people who can have great relationships with their friends and families to be so toxic when they're at work? What shifts when they get around their team or other people in their organization?

These reoccurring questions have been with me for so long that I had to find the answers.

In this section of the book, I'm going to explore what causes good people to become bad leaders. By doing this, we can hopefully make the unconscious conscious, become more self-aware of what we are doing and how we are acting with our teams, and avoid the missteps that cause leaders to fail.

You Might Be a Bad Leader If . . .

The other day someone asked me, "What characteristics make a great leader?"

I think the best way to answer that question is to take a look at great leaders who you know personally and observe their leadership. For me, one of those people is my partner from Advoco, Steve. And one example of his leadership came to mind.

Advoco was located in South Carolina, but Steve lived in California. Once a quarter, Steve would visit Advoco—not for any specific reason. He came for a week just to be with people. Every night he was there, he'd be at a brewery or a restaurant, and he'd let the team know where and when

FINDING SIGNIFICANCE

and that they were welcome to join him. This wasn't a mandatory meeting. No one was expected to come—Steve understood they all had lives outside of work. But wherever Steve went, a packed house followed.

This reminded me of something I heard about W.L. Gore, a billion-dollar manufacturing company with one of the most unique corporate cultures in the world. They don't have a hierarchy, and leaders are not given an assigned team. Instead, team members choose who they want to follow. As chaotic as this sounds, one team member summed up how simple it actually is: "If you call a meeting and people show up, you're a leader."[1] That was Steve in a nutshell. He called nonmandatory meetings and they were a full house every time. People loved being with him.

And funnily enough, this got me thinking about one of my favorite comedy bits—Jeff Foxworthy's "You Might Be a Redneck If…" It's a classic. If you haven't seen it, check it out on YouTube. Foxworthy has written literally thousands of these jokes, but here are a few of my favorites:

- You might be a redneck if you've ever cut your grass and found a car.
- You might be a redneck if you think the stock market has a fence around it.
- You might be a redneck if your house doesn't have curtains but your truck does.

Yep, that's what popped into my head when someone asked me what makes a great leader. Not the redneck stuff—just the phrasing. I started thinking in terms of "You might be a great leader if…" So, I put together a short list of characteristics I believe make a great leader:

- You might be a great leader if **you inspire people**.
- You might be a great leader if **you have influence**.
- You might be a great leader if **you lead like you are not in charge**.
- You might be a great leader if **you are constantly learning and educating yourself**.

- You might be a great leader if **you challenge your people to be the best they can be**.
- You might be a great leader if **you provide security and safety for your team members**.
- You might be a great leader if **you are driven by the bigger vision and not your own self gains**.

I could go on, but you get the idea. You could add to my list or come up with your own based on great leaders you've had or read about.

After I made my list, I realized this phrasing could work in reverse: "You might be a *bad* leader if…" And this got me thinking about another leader I knew. I won't use his real name here—we'll call him James. James was from the company that acquired Advoco. And he'd visit our offices occasionally just like Steve did. He'd let everyone know he was in town and that he'd be at a specific restaurant for lunch or dinner, but no one would show up.

What was the difference between Steve and James? James led by authority—a *me* mentality instead of *we*. Part of it, too, was the tone when James would visit. It was like he was gracing us with his presence. And people were not interested in spending time with him.

This led to my first Foxworthy-style truth about bad leaders: You might be a bad leader if people only spend time with you because they have to. I put together a few more of these phrases based on the research I did on leadership, my own experience, and lots of conversations with friends and colleagues.

You might be a bad leader if you don't recognize and thank your team for their work.

When a project at work succeeds, a bad leader gladly takes the credit. If a project fails, though, they have no problem blaming it on their team. They're slow to give praise and quick to find fault. And they rarely show gratitude for their team's contributions.

You might be a bad leader if you don't provide a vision for success.

Team members want to know what success looks like in two distinct areas. First, they want a clear sense of what success looks like for the organization. They want to know why the company exists, where it's headed, what it wants to accomplish, and how it makes a positive difference in people's lives. That gives meaning to the effort and time they give to the company.

Second, they want to know what success looks like in their specific role. Not only does that give them clarity for setting goals and focusing their energy, it also shows them how important they are to the team. It says, *Here's why we need you. When you accomplish these tasks, the team is more likely to win.*

A bad leader doesn't provide either of those visions of success. Under a bad leader, the team doesn't know where they're headed, how important they are, or why their work matters.

You might be a bad leader if you sanction incompetence.

Bad leaders let incompetence slide—particularly if it serves their interests. Maybe there's a salesman who never hits his numbers, but because he's loyal to the bad leader, he gets a pass. In some cases, the bad leader is just lazy and doesn't feel like putting in the work that it takes to consistently root out poor performance. This is horrible for team morale because it sanctions incompetence. It tells the team that it's okay to underperform. This mentality will spread quickly throughout a team, further weakening morale and creating apathetic team members.

You might be a bad leader if you leave conflicts unresolved.

Bad leaders mishandle conflict in one of two ways. The first way is they stifle conflict before it's resolved. They know that there's tension between team members, but rather than dealing with it, they focus on keeping the peace. They shut the arguments down and encourage everyone to move on. This leaves the conflict festering and unresolved.

You Might Be a Bad Leader If . . .

Second, bad leaders ignore conflict. They let their teams bicker and gossip. They don't encourage resolution or peace. In a lot of cases, they make it even worse by joining in the gossip themselves.

Conflict isn't bad. It allows you to challenge each other and solve problems. But it has to be done with the intent of finding resolution—not just attacking.

A friend of mine works for a software company and he recently went to a meeting with the CEO called "Things We Could Be Doing Better." He was excited about this, and he came up with three big issues to talk about. Well, it didn't go well. The CEO got mad and started yelling at my friend for bringing up the issues. After the meeting, his leader called him into his office, and my friend got yelled at again. "What'd you think you're doing?" his leader said, "You're not supposed to tell him these things."

I've heard this story over and over—leaders don't want real conflict and healthy arguments. They just want to be told how awesome they're doing.

My daughter worked for a company where she had to fill out a report every week telling her leader about her weekly high and her weekly low. For her weekly low, she was honest and mentioned a real issue she was facing. Her leader called her into his office and told her not to mention things like that. It could get him in trouble. Turns out, this was happening company-wide. Anytime someone was too honest, they were told to tone it down. It became a joke among the team members—and a lot of them would just write "nothing comes to mind" for their weekly low. That's the result of bad leaders. They don't want real conflict. They prefer to keep the peace. But that just leaves issues simmering beneath the surface.

You might be a bad leader if you're irritable all the time.

Not surprisingly, bad leaders also come across as highly irritable. They don't want to be bothered for anything. Since they're not open to other ideas from anyone else, they despise being asked questions and avoid it as much as possible. Under a bad leader, the organization becomes stunted because of the lack of innovative and free-flowing ideas.

You might be a bad leader if you lack self-confidence.

Though they act supremely confident, a toxic leader has no confidence in themselves. Consequently, they also find it extremely difficult to trust team members. Because of this insecurity, tough problems are often ignored or swept under the carpet. A strong, confident leader invites challenges because they know they can handle them. Either that or they know they have to act, regardless of how they feel. Bad leaders don't want to be challenged, and they hide from situations that might reveal their shortcomings.

You might be a bad leader if you believe in symbols over substance.

These symbols might include things like priority parking spots for executives, meetings that make leaders feel important but don't serve any real purpose, and leaders placing their own portraits and stories of accomplishments around the workplace.

I could go on and on with this list about what bad leaders do, but the real point of this is to get you thinking. Is there anything you'd add to this list? Maybe it's a behavior you've experienced firsthand, or maybe it's a "bad leader" tendency you have.

As I go through the list, the part that strikes me is most leaders don't even know they're doing these things. They're so caught up in the moment or the pressure of being a leader that they just resort to bad behaviors they've seen other leaders do. They assume that's what leadership is.

In my research, I found that over 90% of people say they've worked for an asshole. As troubling as that is, it gets even more alarming when you think about what this means for up-and-coming leaders: They will inevitably model the behaviors of the leaders above them, and more than nine out of ten of them have experienced really bad leadership. So, they feel they need to act in a similar way to succeed. Then the leaders below them feel that way. And the cycle continues.

Success Is Not the Problem

I wish I didn't have to say this, but this was the easiest chapter for me to write. It wasn't hard to come up with examples of what makes a bad leader. When you stop and think about what causes a leader to fail, it's usually easy to see, and everyone knows it except, unfortunately, the leader with the bad behavior. It's just like the story of the emperor with no clothes. Everyone knew he was naked, except the emperor.

To be honest, thinking about this makes me sad because, as I've talked about throughout the book, it doesn't have to be this way.

Just the other day I was talking with one of my former leaders and posed this question to him: Why do you think leaders fail?

His immediate response was, "Ego. Ego is always the enemy after all."

I responded, "Yes, ego can be the enemy, but how does it manifest itself? What actions action would you say are signs of a bad leader?"

And that's when the floodgates opened and the conversation got deeper. Why? Because we got past the easy, cliché answers about why leaders fail. We've all heard them a thousand times. Ego. Power. Money. Success. Say one of those and everyone nods their heads and the conversation is basically over. Unless you press a little like I did. Then you get closer to the truth. Bad leadership is about bad behaviors. And what brings about those behaviors is a complex web of cause and effect, which we'll discuss in the next chapter.

But I want to make it clear that it's not a title, position, or paycheck that *makes* you a bad leader. The root causes for every bad leader existed long before they achieved success. Success is not the problem!

Sara Blakely, one of the youngest self-made female billionaires, said it best when she said: "Money and success just make you more of who you already are. I don't think it changes you. If you were insecure before you had a bunch of money or success, you become more insecure. If you were a jerk, you become a bigger jerk. If you were kind, you become kinder. If you were generous, you become more generous. All it does is hold a magnifying glass up to who you are."[2]

So, the truth about a lot of bad leaders is they were jerks before the success, the fancy title, and the paycheck. Those things just made their characteristics more obvious. And the same goes for great leaders. I think that makes a lot of sense, but it doesn't answer a big question: What makes *good people* become bad leaders? If money and success aren't the problem, then what is? That's what I want to talk about next.

There are five pressure points every leader faces. We have to understand what they are and how they influence us because they're the reason good people become bad leaders.

Chapter 11

The 5 Pressure Points

Back in chapter 1, we went over some survey questions about leaders. If you don't remember, let me give you a quick refresher. I sent out some questions to people in my network asking them what they thought about bad leaders and great leaders.

One of the questions I asked was, "What do you think your *organization* wants from its leaders?" Here's a sample of the most popular answers:

- Productivity
- Loyalty
- Bottom-line results
- Deliver the results
- Organization
- Numbers person
- Honesty
- Yes person
- Make money

Now, here are two other questions I asked about what *teams* and *employees* want from their leaders: "What characteristics make leaders great?" and, "What traits do you most appreciate in a leader?" As you might expect, there was a lot of overlap with the answers to these two questions. Here's a sampling:

- Empathy
- Respect
- Visionary
- Transparent
- Engaging
- Compassionate
- Trustworthy
- Willing to listen

The 5 Pressure Points

Notice anything? When you look at what people think organizations want from leaders and what teams want, there's no overlap. It's a whole different set of qualities. And in most cases, that's exactly how it is at companies.

So, what does this mean? It means leaders are under a lot of pressure because they're trying to keep two very different groups of people happy. And it's that pressure that makes good people become bad leaders.

My Confession

Okay, I have to admit something, and this isn't easy for me. I was fired for the first time in my career by the company that acquired Advoco. I've mentioned that I left and knew it was time to move on, which is true, but I haven't said exactly why.

Honestly, it's a hard thing to come clean about because here I am writing a book about leadership, and I've set myself up to supposedly be some great leader who's been in Forbes magazine, helped lead his company to become South Carolina's number one best place to work, and has been sought after by huge companies to solve some of their biggest challenges. But I was fired. Let go. Told my services will no longer be needed.

How could I go from the top to "you're fired"?

It all goes back to what I call the *leadership pressure points*. Pressure is an amazing thing. When multiple forces are working against each other, what happens? Something has to give.

We see this with water pipes. The pressure gets too high, something bursts, and we've got a mess on our hands.

It's the same when our leadership brand doesn't align with our organization's brand. And that's what happened with me.

When Advoco was acquired, I was 100% on board. With the new company's resources, I thought the sky was the limit—we could double the business. A lot of people laughed at me. They knew what happens to the people at the top in an acquisition. I did too, but I stayed hopeful. I was actually excited, and I made a choice to believe that it could work out.

To me, it felt like this was the next phase for Advoco, and I thought I could align myself with how the acquiring company did business.

Obviously, things went south. Remember the Working Genius framework? I'm a discerner and a galvanizer. So, I want to be trusted and heard. But the company who acquired us is a massive corporation, and they're not in the business of listening to or trusting employees. That meant I spent every day in my working frustration.

Our employees were upset with how the new company handled the transition, and lots of them were leaving. I tried to tell the acquiring company to listen to my employees—they just want to be heard. Just getting it off their chests will go a long way to keeping some of these people. But they wouldn't do it. They'd say, "We're a big company. This is how we do things."

I also had to fight to get the new company to deliver on what they promised our team. We were told we'd get specific compensation and titles, but that didn't go smoothly. Thankfully, it worked out for the most part. But that's only because we—the leaders—stuck around to see it through. I knew of leaders from other companies who took the acquisition checks and ran off before the merger. Their teams got screwed over. In fact, some of my team members were in meetings with them where these people from other companies would say, "How'd Advoco get that? We didn't get that!"

Throughout all this, I'd meet regularly with a rep from the acquiring company. He'd say to me: "I've seen this movie fifty times—it always ends the same. Doesn't matter how hard you try to fight, this is always how it goes." Basically, he was telling me to surrender now. Fighting was futile.

It all came to a head when they wanted 60% of my time to be billable. There was no structure in place for that to happen. And it's not how Advoco did business. I couldn't get anyone to care or listen to me, though. Looking back, I know it was naïve to think I could've changed their minds. They wanted billable resources, period. That's how they did business. They'd never consider changing because of me.

Well, I overreacted and went to 0% billable. I was doing the work, but just giving other people the credit. I was trying to get their attention and open up a conversation. Instead, I was told, "Your services are no longer needed." Whoops.

I realize now that my leadership brand was in deep conflict with their organization's brand. I had a *we* mentality. Teamwork. That applied to clients too. I wanted to help them solve their problems without worrying about complicated billing codes and who should get credit for helping them. But the new company had a *me* mentality. That was reflected in every area of their business—from policies to internal communications to overall culture.

You can see how pressure would build in that situation. It was only a matter of time until something burst. I was trying to live out my leadership brand while they wanted me to conform to their brand. Something had to give.

I'll be real with you: It was embarrassing. Not getting let go—that was inevitable. I'm embarrassed by how hopeful I was that it could work out. But you know what? That's my leadership brand. I believe the future can be better. I chose to adapt to a new situation. I couldn't have done it any other way, and I'm glad I gave it a shot.

It was also a learning experience. Without it, I wouldn't have clearly seen how outside pressures can work against a leadership brand. And I wouldn't have come up with the five pressure points. Let's take a look at those now.

Pressure Point 1: Your Organization

Simply put, your organization wants something from you—certain behaviors and results. Sometimes they make that clear, and sometimes it's left unsaid and you have to figure it out based on the organization's culture. (If you're unsure about what your organization wants, just look at why they reward people. That'll tell you all you need to know.) Either way, what your organization wants can quickly conflict with your leadership brand.

FINDING SIGNIFICANCE

Pressure Point 2: Your Leader

Your leader is facing all the same pressure points you are—and it's likely more intense for them. You want their guidance, but they might be more lost than you—especially if they're not conscious of their leadership brand and their ego. If they're ego-driven and reactionary, it's more likely they'll be a tough pressure point for you.

Pressure Point 3: Your Team

If you've developed your leadership brand well, what your team wants from you will probably line up with your brand. But even if that's the case, each member of your team is different and needs to be treated in a unique way (see the Working Genius section in chapter 6), and that can put pressure on you. And if your organization's culture is toxic, your team members can easily internalize that and want something from you that conflicts with your brand.

Pressure Point 4: Your Family

You may not have thought about it, but what your family wants can affect your leadership brand. What do they want? Most likely your time. They want *you*. And there's the pressure point—because your organization, leaders, and team want your time too. What gets people in trouble is when they work too much, trying to live up to the demands of their organization and leader. Your family doesn't want a zoned-out, zombie version of you, either. They'd like you to have some energy left to give them. And that can be tough when you've got a high-pressure job.

Pressure Point 5: Your Investors/Owners/Board

This pressure point is unique because of how variable the intensity can be. If you're high up in a large, established organization, the pressure can be intense. If you're more mid-level, you may barely feel it. But if you're at a small startup, you'll feel this at just about any level. It also varies depending on things like whether you're at a publicly traded corporation, government agency, or nonprofit organization. And if you're running a small business, you're probably the investor, owner, and board. Believe it

The 5 Pressure Points

or not, you can be at odds with yourself here. As an investor, you might want to grow the business. But as a husband and father, you might not.

Even though this pressure point will look a little different for everyone, it's basically the same at its core: It's pressure from people with a lot of influence over you and your company. They can withhold funding, drive share prices up or down, or change the direction of the organization.

Pressure Points Exercise

Alright, let's do a quick exercise. Get a pen ready and use the spaces provided below to write.

First, let's rewrite those words you chose as your leadership brand back in chapter 2.

What Do I Want My Leadership Brand to Be?

1. _____
2. _____
3. _____
4. _____
5. _____

Now, write down three words or phrases you think your organization, leaders, team, family, and investors/board want from you. These can be traits (like loyalty, productivity, empathy) or action phrases (like hit my numbers, listen to their ideas, spend time with them).

What Does My Organization Want from Me?

1. _____
2. _____
3. _____

What Do My Leaders Want from Me?

1. _____
2. _____
3. _____

What Does My Team Want from Me?

1. _____
2. _____
3. _____

What Does My Family Want from Me?

1. _____
2. _____
3. _____

What Do My Investors/Owners/Board Members Want from Me?

1. _____
2. _____
3. _____

Okay, now take a look at your five leadership brand words and compare them with the words from your five pressure points. How well do they line up? If they're pretty close, then congratulations! You're probably in your sweet spot, and you've got a good balance at work and at home.

But if your lists aren't aligning, that's okay. There are more people in this situation than not. And they might never align—there will likely always be some tension between your leadership brand and your pressure points. But that doesn't mean you have to fail or become a bad leader.

The power in this exercise is in understanding the forces at play. Once again, you're making the unconscious conscious. The win here isn't that you'll have perfect harmony. The win is that you'll be fully aware of the forces at work. Understanding the five pressure points will help you see what you're up against. That in itself is a huge step forward. It makes it easier to figure out what's wrong when you're feeling uneasy.

You might begin to see, for instance, that your leadership brand will always be in conflict with what your organization wants from you. This may not be good news, but it's the reality of your situation. And you can be empowered by simply naming what is happening. Maybe you felt tense and uncertain in your career but didn't understand why. With knowledge of the pressure points, you can grasp what's going on.

With that knowledge comes a choice. Here are the options:
1. Leave the company.
2. Stay and try to change the culture.
3. Stay and try to work around the culture.

Most people can't easily leave their jobs. And most people don't have the power to significantly change the culture. That means a lot of people are left with option three—they have to figure out how to work within a culture that doesn't resonate with them. That might not be ideal, but it's where a lot of us end up.

If you're in this kind of situation, it's important that you *choose* to stay. You might think, *I have no choice. I'm stuck here.* No, you're not. It might not be practical to leave, but the truth is, you can always do it. You could quit tomorrow. Fear is keeping you from leaving your job, and that's completely normal and understandable. It doesn't make you a bad person. We crave security and familiarity, and quitting a job comes with risks. But if you really feel like it's time to go, doing a quick fear exercise might help.

I learned this exercise while working with Scribe Media. I hired them a few years ago to help me write this book, and one of the first things they did was sit me down and tell me, "Fear will keep you from completing this book." So, we wrote down reasons I'd be afraid of finishing. We made things conscious, and the truth is, 90% of what we fear never happens.

So, let's do that now. What could go wrong if you quit your job? Your income drops? You have to skip a vacation or hold off on buying a new car? Or maybe you'd be embarrassed if you failed?

Even if those things happened, wouldn't you be glad you tried? You attempted to shape your destiny. If things went terribly wrong, couldn't you get a job somewhere as a last resort? Could you tap into an emergency fund or a retirement account to pay your mortgage?

My point is, even if the worst happened, couldn't you survive it? In the end, it's often riskier to keep ignoring that stirring in your chest than it is to leave your job.

But what if you like the people you work with or the cause that your company fights for? What if part of you wants to stay in spite of the fact that you don't align with your leaders or organization? If that's the case, you have to ask yourself: Can I survive if I stay? Can I really make this work?

I know someone who's been amazing at making things work at companies that don't necessarily line up with his leadership brand. His name's Javier, and he's a longtime business colleague and good friend of mine. He's one of the best leaders I've ever worked with, and I've always admired his tenacity and ability to work within any framework or culture that's thrown his way.

Javier has worked for about ten different bosses throughout his career, and many of them have been total jerks. So, how does he do it? How does he continue to live his leadership brand while the organization and people around him want him to be different?

When I asked Javier those questions, his answer revealed a lot about his mindset. He said, "I listen first to really understand the new culture. If we have an alignment on certain key points, I emphasize those. If I find a disagreement point, then I take a neutral position on that until I can create a logical story to modify it or convince myself it's not that bad."

When I think about Javier's brand, the one thing that has always stuck out for me is his ability to not react. He takes time to get to know the new leader or organization and figure out where there's common ground. Once he understands how he can be effective, then he goes all in. But he's willing to wait. He reacts on his timeline and when he feels the time is right.

One favorite story of mine is when I first met Javier at the company we both worked for. He was head of development, and I was just appointed VP of product management. I was new to the position, and I knew I would need to get along with the head of development if we were ever going to get things done. So I reached out to Javier.

He congratulated me on the new position and then he said something to me that I will never forget: "I will do anything in my power to help you be successful if you agree to one thing." Not knowing what he might ask, I said, "Sure, I'll consider what you have to say."

He said, "Don't try and hire my product specialist, Lee, away from my team." I had no idea who Lee was at the time, so I gladly agreed, and Javier and I became fast friends.

Knowing Javier now, I'm sure he would have supported Lee if he wanted to pursue a new position. But he didn't want anyone poaching Lee away and breaking up his team.

What I came to learn about Javier as a leader is he is fiercely loyal to his team. He would do anything to defend and support them. He worked hard to create space for them to do their work and not get swept up in corporate politics. He encourage each of them to find their significance and help them become the leader people were happy to see.

As I followed Javier's career over the years, what I noticed was that no matter who was in charge of the company or what the organization wanted from him, Javier was able to get along with them as long as they respected his team. I'm not sure if his team understood just how much he did for them. But based on the incredibly low turnover on Javier's teams, I'd say they knew they had a great leader.

When I think about Javier, I can't help but think about a passage in the Bible from John 10: "The good shepherd lays down his life for the sheep. The hired hand is not the shepherd....So when he sees the wolf coming, he abandons the sheep and runs away."[1]

Great leaders lay down their life for their teams. They protect them and always put them ahead of themselves. The hired hands, aka bad leaders, don't risk anything. They run when pushed. They spend more time worrying about themselves than their team.

Javier taught me an important lesson: You can have a fulfilling career even at a company that doesn't line up with your leadership brand. It all depends on your goals. And that's an important lesson to learn because no organization will perfectly line up with your brand. For Javier, his teams were so important to him that he wanted to stay and fight for them—despite the fact that he sometimes clashed with the company or its leadership.

So, you don't have to always escape the organization when it doesn't line up with your brand. Again, everyone's situation is different, so I can't tell you what you should do without knowing your specifics. It really boils down to what you want and what's healthy for you in the long term. Sometimes you can stay. But sometimes it's best to go—especially when the culture is overwhelmingly at odds with who you want to be as a leader.

Culture

For me, it wasn't possible to stay in a situation where the organization and my brand didn't align. And what this boiled down to was culture. Going back to the Working Genius, if I felt like I wasn't being heard, I didn't do well. That's because I'm a galvanizer. I crave to be heard, I'm crushed when I'm ignored. And organizations with a top-down leadership style aren't good at listening. So when I found myself in that type of company, it was impossible for me to thrive.

I want to dig in on culture because nothing can influence leadership more than an organization's culture. Culture dictates how people act and how they lead. Most of us aren't Javier. We can't stand against the cultural current—eventually we get swept right in.

So, carefully consider your organization's culture, because there's a good chance that whatever your leaders do now is what you'll be doing soon if you keep moving up the ranks.

What Is Culture?

I think culture is one of the most overused and least-understood terms out there.

Culture is not something you say or write on a wall. It's not the core values you've got somewhere on your website or hanging in your lunchroom.

Culture isn't what your leadership team says it is. It's what they do. Culture is always driven from the top down.

Ultimately, culture is a feeling. You sense it in the air. It's the unwritten rules of how people are supposed to act. That's a little vague, I know. So let me give you a concrete way to determine a company's culture: *Pay attention to what a company rewards.*

That's culture. Ignore everything a company says and watch what they reward. That will tell you everything you need to know.

The company says it puts people over profits, but it worships the sales team and overlooks egregious behavior from the top salespeople. That's a revenue-driven culture.

The company says we're a culture of *we*, but they promote the asshole who is all about *me*. That's a results-driven culture.

The company says they value risk-taking, but every time they try something new and it fails, they look for someone to blame. That's a fearful and risk-averse culture.

The company says they value honesty, straight shooters, and healthy conflict, but all the leaders got their titles by being "yes people" and toeing the company line. That's a loyalty-driven culture.

You can't hide culture. Everyone knows what it is.

I wish companies would just be honest about their cultures. But they can't. We have to tell ourselves a noble story even when the truth is staring us in the face.

A company might say they value everyone equally. But then they have things like Presidents Clubs, where people who are already top earners get rewarded with expensive perks. So, they separate the "in crowd" from the "just do your job" crowd.

At Advoco, our culture was work hard, play hard. So, what did that mean? We believed that results mattered, but we also didn't take ourselves too seriously. We wanted the journey to be fun. For us, fun meant having passion for what we did. Passion for learning, passion for our teammates, passion for our customers. And of course, passion for partying and having a good time. "Work hard" meant we had a responsibility. A responsibility to the business for results. A responsibility to the customer to solve their most pressing problems, and a responsibility to be the best at what we did.

Let's do a quick exercise. Write down three things your company rewards. These could be words or phrases, things like "loyalty" or "generating revenue." It might help to think about who gets promoted and why.

Things My Organization Rewards

1. _____

2. _____

3. _____

Take a look at that list—that's your company's culture. Does it resonate with your leadership brand?

In management expert Peter Drucker's immortal words, "Culture eats strategy for breakfast." But what does that actually mean?

It means culture dictates how work gets done because it shapes the work atmosphere and profoundly impacts employees. Companies can set strategies all they want, but it's the culture that will determine whether the strategy gets implemented on time, on budget, and most importantly, with excellence.

Knowing this, do you think your company's culture is setting the company up for success? Do you think it's setting you up for success? Do you see your company as a place you could become a great leader?

Cultures Change

Cultures evolve over time. But sadly, they almost always go from good to bad or bad to worse. Why is that?

In a lot of cases, it's because they become more risk-averse over time. And that's because the people who lead them become more risk-averse.

A new company has nothing to lose. They're open to new ideas and willing to pivot constantly. And it's the same for young leaders at a new company. But as a company and its leaders get more successful, they have more to lose. So, they take fewer risks and are less open to new ideas.

The culture becomes less innovative, and this affects who they hire. They look for—and attract—"yes people" who are good at following rules instead of creative people who are good at breaking them.

Playing it safe and being loyal become entrenched values. The company rewards people who exhibit them with promotions. So, these behaviors become self-perpetuating across leadership and teams, and that's when the culture spirals downward. At that point, it's very hard to turn it around.

That's a common way a culture can change, but it's not the only way. The point is that cultures tend to change in a negative direction. But no matter what kind of culture you're in, remember this: Culture doesn't just change—it changes *you*. So, you have to decide what you're willing to tolerate and how much pressure you can withstand. You don't want to compromise your brand. Can you be the leader people are happy to see in the middle of your current culture? Could you use your influence to change the culture for the better? Those are the questions you need to answer.

There Can Be Only One

Have you seen the *Highlander* movies? The basic plot is that some aliens get sent to Earth as a punishment. They have the ability to live forever on Earth, but the catch is, only one of them will win that privilege. So, they go around fighting each other because—as the famous tagline says—"There can be only one."

It's the same with company culture—there can only be one. That's why acquisitions usually go so badly. One culture collides with another culture, and the hope is that they can somehow merge. But it's just not possible. The acquiring company's culture will almost always win out.

The company that acquired Advoco used to say, "We are a culture of cultures." What BS. Whatever that company valued and rewarded would soon be what was expected of us, and that'd be the end of Advoco's culture. And that's exactly what happened.

You might get pockets of people resisting and trying to create their own culture, but ultimately, one wins out.

But what about my friend Javier? Didn't he successfully create another culture? No, he was successful at protecting his team—shielding them from the culture. And the company tolerated him. Why? Because he had low turnover, put out quality work, and made the company more profitable. So, you can have a sort of safe haven within a company if you've got a strong leader who gets results. The caveat is, the company has to value those results. If Javier's main accomplishment was awesome feedback about his team's mental health, his company wouldn't have tolerated his outlier leadership style.

What I'm saying is, you'll have to play the game and understand what your company's culture wants from you. But you can still lead in a way you can be proud of—as long as you keep your leaders happy. You won't change the culture. You'll simply be allowed to operate within it. Because in the end, there's only one culture.

Understand Where You're Headed

Now let's look at an example of someone who wasn't able to operate within a culture that conflicted with her leadership brand. This is sort of the opposite of Javier's story.

When I was at Infor, the executive board decided there were too many men in leadership at the partner level. They needed to hire a woman. But they didn't understand what type of personality they needed. (This is why tests like DISC and Working Genius are so important. See chapter 6.) They also didn't understand their own culture and who would be a good fit. Once the "female" box was checked, they made the hire.

The woman they hired was great. I loved her. She believed in building teams and accountability. She didn't like a lot of hierarchy—she led by inspiring, not by leveraging her title. She praised people and helped them get better. And they fired her within six months.

The bottom line was she wasn't a bully. And this was a company that rewarded bullies who hit their metrics by any means possible. For her leadership style to be effective, she needed some time to build trust. The board wasn't patient enough for that. They also didn't understand her—she just didn't fit the culture. And this woman, to her credit, wasn't willing to compromise who she was or how she'd treat her team. If the board was after genuine diversity, they would have listened to this woman and tried to understand her leadership style. But that's not what they wanted. They wanted a clone of themselves who checked a diversity box.

So, the board learned their lesson and hired, quite frankly, a bully. I'm not qualified to diagnose anyone, but I'd bet money this woman was a narcissist. At least the board understood who they were and what kind of company they were running. Over the next three years, she ran off most of the sales team, replaced them with people like her, alienated the customers, and ruined the business. Infor is a shell of itself now.

The lesson here is that you need to understand how high up in a company you want to go. Most people think, *All the way to the top!* But if you're not aligned with your organization or its leadership, going to the top isn't going to work. Javier survived and thrived because he stayed at the mid-manager level. When you reach the executive board, you'd better conform to their expectations. That's just another layer to think about as you consider how the five pressure points will impact your leadership brand.

Before you set yourself in a certain direction—to be the CEO of Company X, let's say—you should ask yourself some questions. How will this position conflict with your family's needs? How will the board and investors expect you to treat your team? What will they want you to prioritize? What will the organization want from you in terms of time and expectations? Understanding the company's culture will help you answer a lot of these questions. That, in turn, will help you know whether you're headed in the right direction—a direction that allows you to live out your leadership brand values without being crushed by the five pressure points.

Once you get to that place—and I believe you can—you'll face another challenge: Do you plateau, rest on your laurels, coast into retirement? Or do you keep pushing to the next level? I hope your answer is always to keep pushing. If that's what you want, you'll need to understand that what got you here is not going to get you there.

Chapter 12

What Got You Here Is Not Going to Get You There

I mentioned that chapter 10—"You Might Be a Bad Leader If…"—was the easiest chapter for me to write. Well, I believe this is one of the most important chapters.

It's easy to talk about what a great leader looks like.

It's easy to talk about what might cause you to fail.

But I'll tell you what's hard: To look in the mirror and say, "It's me. I'm what's holding me back. I have to change."

Our egos tell us we're pretty awesome, so why change?

I first heard the phrase "what got you here is not going to get you there" from author and speaker John Maxwell. He didn't come up with it, but he saw the wisdom in it. The idea always stuck with me for two reasons: First, it forced me to relook at myself and what I was doing as a leader. Second, it summed up the biggest reason I saw the leaders around me start to fail.

The Story of Scott

As Advoco started to grow, I was always looking for help and support from others business leaders. I figured if I could find someone who had already blazed a trail before me, why not learn from their experiences? That person for me was Scott. I first met Scott when I was working at Datastream. During our tenure, Scott decided to leave Datastream and start his own business with another colleague. I remember watching his business grow and wanting to do what he was doing.

Once I left Datastream to join my partners Steve and Paul at Advoco, I would call Scott up on a regular basis to get advice on challenges I was dealing with.

In our fourth year, we were looking to take the company to the next level, so I asked Scott if he would meet with me. He graciously accepted. During that meeting, I was asking him all kinds of questions around structure and what I could do to build the right team. And then out of nowhere, Scott stopped me and looked me in the eyes and said, "Do you know what your problem is?"

I looked back and said, "No, that's why I'm here." He smiled and then pointed his finger at me and said, "*You* are the problem."

I was pretty shocked. "I'm the problem? How can I be the problem? I'm the one trying to solve all these problems!"

He said, "That's the problem. You need to let your team solve them. You need to challenge your team to be the solution, not you." (In other words, stop trying to be the hero.)

Now, I'm not sure how you would have taken this, but at first, I was hurt. I'm here trying to solve all these challenges—why's he pointing fingers at me?

But the more I reflected and stood in the moment, I knew he was right.

What got us here was not going to get us to the next level.

They say the success of a team is only as good as the sum of its parts, and if that team was just me, it wasn't going to have much success.

I needed to empower my team to solve challenges. I needed to be more open to their ideas, to let them explore solutions—not just do what I told them.

We see this every day in business—leaders who believe they have to be in charge of everything. They have to be the answer to every situation. Some do this because they feel like they'll look weak or won't be needed if they don't. Others do it because that's how they had to be early in their careers—either to get ahead at their company or because they were entrepreneurs and everything was always on their shoulders. And it worked. But it doesn't work forever—what got them here won't get them there.

To become the leader people are happy to see, we need to embrace growth. We need to challenge our own ideas—even the ones that brought us success.

Adam Grant wrote a great book on this topic called *Think Again*. In it, he examines what causes great leaders and great companies to fail. He says that we put a ton of importance on intelligence, which is the ability to think and learn. But another set of skills might be more important: the ability to *rethink* and *unlearn*.

Those skills are hard to come by because humans like to feel like they're right. It's comforting for us. So we tend to surround ourselves with people that think like we do, and we seek out ideas that are similar to our own. That makes us feel *more* right, which makes it even harder to rethink our beliefs.

When we do encounter people who disagree with us, our egos jump in to protect us. We dig our heels in and fight back, rather than seeing an opportunity to learn.

And it can get even worse if we're successful. Our egos tell us we didn't get here by listening to other people, so why start now? That's why high achievers can be so resistant to change. Success reinforces all their beliefs and ideas. If you want an entertaining way to see how this can play out, check out *BlackBerry* on Netflix. It's the story of Mike Lazaridis. You might not know his name, but he's the founder of BlackBerry and the creator of its iconic phone.

Most of you probably remember BlackBerrys. But for those of you born after 1990, let me fill you in real quick. BlackBerrys were everywhere. Every big-name business tycoon had one, Obama had one, Brad Pitt had one,

Kim Kardashian had one. It was *the* phone—the iPhone before the iPhone. And one feature in particular made it stand out: its keyboard.

BlackBerrys had actual physical keyboards. And you'd type with your thumbs while each button made a satisfying little click.

Well, when the first iPhone came out, it didn't have a physical keyboard. And Mike Lazaridis thought this was nuts. Obviously, people loved the iPhone, but Mike was confident that touchscreens were a passing fad. In an interview in 2008, he was asked about the most exciting mobile trend. Here's what he said:

> "Full Qwerty keyboards. I'm sorry, it really is. I'm not making this up. People are…coming into the stores and they want to be able to do Facebook and they want to be able to do instant messaging and they want to be able to do email and they ask for those features thinking that they're going to get another flip phone and they're walking out with a (BlackBerry) Curve or a Pearl because they're the best devices for doing those kinds of activities. And so what is the defining factor? The keyboard."[1]

Think about this. It's 2008, not even a year after the iPhone came out, and Mike is saying the hottest trend in mobile is…keyboards. They'd been around for years! Apple had just launched a ground-breaking phone packed with never-before-seen innovations: iTunes, Google Maps, the first good mobile web browser (Safari), a touchscreen that seemed like magic—that's the short list. Apple's also a month away from launching its App Store, which Mike had to know about. And yet, the hottest trend is keyboards.

This is clearly a situation where a high-achieving individual is blinded by their success. He kept clinging to the idea that what got him here (keyboards) was going to get him there (domination of the mobile market).

But it didn't. Instead, BlackBerry failed miserably. They went from the number one phone in the world to losing their entire market share. They were once valued at over $80 billion, trading at more than $145 a share. Now they trade at about $2 a share, and they don't make phones at all.

Failing the Right Way

How could Mike and his team have prevented this from happening? There's not a simple answer to that. To compete with the iPhone, they would have needed to make a long string of great decisions. But I can confidently say this: Focusing on keyboards was a massive mistake. Mike retreated to his comfort zone and dragged the whole company there with him. What he needed to do was *rethink* and *unlearn*. He should have thrown out every idea he had about phones and asked himself, *If I'd never made a phone before and decided to make a brand-new one today, how would I do that?*

Instead, he and his team bet that the iPhone would be a passing fad. They decided to wait for it to fail when what they should have been doing is innovating like crazy. It's like they retreated to the castle, pulled up the bridge, and waited for Apple to go away.

The problem here isn't that BlackBerry failed—failure is part of business—it's *how* they failed.

Let's look at a better way to take a business loss. In 1994, Richard Branson launched Virgin Cola and made it clear he wanted to take down Coke and Pepsi. To kick off his campaign in the US, he drove a tank over three tons of Coke cans in Times Square. As if that wasn't enough, he then pointed the tank's gun at Coke's huge sign and "fired." Thanks to pyrotechnics he'd had his team install the night before, it looked like the sign blew up. This is the opposite of retreating to the castle and locking the gate. If you're going to fail—and Virgin Cola eventually did—this is a better way to do it.

Before it was discontinued, Virgin Cola had a lot of success, outselling Coke and Pepsi in the UK, and flying off the shelves in Targets across America. But that success led to its eventual failure because it got Coke's attention. Coke used some clever bullying tactics to keep it off the shelves in major US retailers. In spite of being the superior product—Virgin Cola repeatedly won blind taste tests—it disappeared by the early 2000s.

Branson took the failure as an opportunity to learn. Here's what he told Guy Raz on the *How I Built This* podcast:

> "The problem was that, you know, we didn't have something completely unique. We had a great brand. But Coke had a great brand. The taste of the Cola was maybe marginally better. But it was neither here nor there.
>
> So since then what I learned from that was only to go into businesses where we were palpably better than all the competition."[2]

The Paradox of Success

The difference between Mike Lazaridis and Richard Branson boils down to this: Mike failed by playing it safe. Richard failed by taking calculated risks.

You might be thinking that they both failed either way, so what's the difference? It's this: You don't learn by playing it safe. You don't grow. And you actually become more likely to fail in a significant way. Virgin has hundreds of operations and products across five industries. They operate in retail, travel, media, telecommunications, and banking. That's because they've continually experimented with new ventures. Meanwhile, BlackBerry has faded into a small cybersecurity company.

We have to be willing to try new things. We have to keep pushing ourselves to explore new ideas. For so many leaders, it's their inability to rethink how they've always done things that sabotages their careers.

So, why do we resist change?

Because of the paradox of success. The more successful we become, the more likely we are to believe our ideas, choices, and behaviors made us successful. So we stop looking outside ourselves for answers. We stop listening to other voices. We look backward—at our past decisions—to figure out what to do next.

What we're really thinking is, *I got here by listening to myself. And I'll get to the next level by doing the same thing.*

When you start thinking thoughts like this, you're about to plateau. One way to figure out if that's where you're at is to watch how you respond to criticism. Do you immediately get defensive and think that there's no truth in the criticism? Do you try to discredit the other person rather than consider what they're saying?

All of us in the workplace delude ourselves about our achievements, our status, and contributions. We try and inflate the false self. Stay humble instead. Understand that, yes, part of your success is because of your behavior, but another huge part is because of how open-minded you were to new ideas, how hungry you were to learn and grow—not to mention a good deal of luck and help from other people.

If you feel like you've hit a plateau, you might be wondering how to change or if change is even possible. For those of us deep into our careers or just set in our ways, turning things around can feel almost hopeless. I can assure you it's never too late for a new start. In the next section, we'll explore the question, "Can a leader change?" And we'll learn valuable lessons from a couple leaders who completely transformed themselves.

Part IV

Can a Leader Change?

Chapter 13

An Unexpected Transformation

In 2019, I started getting serious about writing this book. I'd been writing Marty's Minutes and speaking for years, and people would always say, "You've got to write a book!" After hearing that over and over, I finally thought, *Okay, I'll do it*. I love to learn. My working geniuses are discerner and galvanizer. It just made sense.

To make it official, I announced it on stage at one of Advoco's conferences. That raised the stakes. The crowd was full of people who'd encouraged me to write a book, so once I made that public commitment, I knew I was on the hook to follow through.

The obvious problem was that I'd never written a book before. But leaders are learners, right? If I put in the work, I could figure this out.

I started working with a company called Scribe. They've helped some serious authors put out best sellers, most notably *Can't Hurt Me* by David Goggins. And their process was unique. They didn't write the book for you. They helped you pull the book out of yourself. And then they gave you feedback—including a "Hurt Your Feelings" critique—and helped you shape the book into something that's ready for readers.

Scribe was founded by Tucker Max. If you don't know that name, don't worry about it. I didn't either. But Tucker has sold millions of books. His most famous, *I Hope They Serve Beer in Hell*, was on the New York Times Best Seller list for five years. When I signed up for Scribe, I didn't know Tucker was a best-selling author, had a controversial bad-boy reputation, and made a living telling the world about his frat-boy exploits. The only clue I had came from a buddy of mine. I told him I was going to a class with Tucker Max, and he said, "He was my college hero!" Okay, sure—I had no idea why he said that.

Back in 2019, Scribe's process was more intensive than it is now. It started with a two-day on-site class called Self-Guided Author. And Tucker Max himself led the class in Austin, Texas.

So, there I am in this room with about ten other aspiring authors and Tucker Max. And I was seriously impressed by him. What struck me about him was how good he was with people. I could tell he was super smart. I could also tell he had the ability to be an asshole, but he never was. When people asked questions, he gave incredibly insightful answers. And he'd help them dig deeper into their emotions and draw out more themes and material for their books. He was completely focused on making us better writers.

I found myself thinking, *Who is this guy?* So, I did some research on him, and I was shocked. His whole schtick was that he was an asshole. Literally. Here's the first line on the back cover of his best-selling book: "My name is Tucker Max, and I am an asshole."[1] And he's no run-of-the-mill jerk—his books were sexist, filthy, and borderline sociopathic.

I couldn't believe that the guy who wrote *I Hope They Serve Beer in Hell* was the same guy teaching my writing class.

Let me just give you one example of the kind of guy he was. This is a pretty mild story compared to his other stuff, but it shows you how insane and inconsiderate he could be.

Tucker went to Duke law school, and it was really difficult to get tickets to men's basketball games. So Duke created something called the Campout. Grad students would camp out in tents for a weekend so they could get entered into a lottery to get tickets.

Tucker camped out in style—in an RV on a hill overlooking the tent camp below. He also bought a bullhorn for the occasion. This bullhorn had a one-mile range and had a 110-decibel siren. It was meant for police use.

All day long, Tucker shouted things through the bullhorn at the campers below. Rude, filthy, offensive things. And he didn't stop when the sun went down. He shouted things all night too, keeping everyone at the campsite awake until morning. At one point, the people in the tents gathered at the base of the hill, ready to storm his RV.

Why'd he do it? Why annoy and harass people for no reason? Frat-boy Tucker would've told you it was because he could, because it was fun, because he was a badass who didn't give a shit. But present-day Tucker tells a different story: He did that kind of stuff because he was a mess.

From Warrior to Builder

Even though Tucker grew up with fairly wealthy parents, he had a rough childhood filled with trauma. It wasn't physical or sexual trauma—it was neglect. Tucker's parents divorced when he was one, and his dad was too busy running his restaurants to bother spending time with him. His mom was a flight attendant, and they moved around a lot. She also struggled with alcoholism—she'd start drinking at 10 a.m. and not stop all day. Tucker told me he was alone *a lot*. At four and five years old, he'd be home alone for hours at a time. He said that really messes with your mind.

So, maybe there's a reason he felt the need to shout into that bullhorn at the top of hill. Tucker wanted to be seen and heard. Maybe that's why he wrote books filled with crazy stories. I can't say for sure, but I do know this: Tucker changed. And he put in a lot of work to make that happen.

So how did he go from immature asshole to leader of a successful company?

First, by being curious—he started to wonder what was wrong with him, what made him act the way he did. That led him to seek out professional help, then he did a ton of work in therapy to figure himself out. He did psychoanalysis four times a week for four years. He started meditating. He tried yoga, cognitive behavior therapy, EMDR therapy, and on and on. He even met a shaman who offered to help with crystals and chanting. That seemed to do something for about a year, but he hit a wall there too.

He spent over six years trying to get better. And he definitely made progress, but he always felt like he couldn't get to the core of his issues. He writes, "I could still feel that I had a layer of emotional baggage that I was not reaching. It was either too deep, or my defenses were too strong. I knew I had more work to do…but I didn't know how to do it. So I reached out to my network for help."[2]

That's when he turned to MDMA. Listen, I don't endorse this. It's a drug, and it's not legal in the US. But there's a lot of data that shows how helpful it can be—MDMA cures 70–85% of people suffering from treatment-resistant PTSD.

Tucker used it in a therapeutic setting, and he had a huge breakthrough. He said it's very hard to describe, but he "felt true love…the purest, most deep love I'd ever felt."[3] And he knows how flaky that sounds, but there's just no other way to put it in words.

MDMA is not a psychedelic—you're not tripping or hallucinating. Tucker was mentally sharp the whole time. In fact, maybe too much so. He started talking about how to market MDMA and what the legal red tape would be. This was his way of avoiding emotions. His wife and therapist had to get him to stop intellectualizing and just feel what was happening.

When he did that, all the trauma came up. He didn't have flashbacks like a lot of people do. He had a physical response. His legs shook for hours. He thinks that had something to do with his messed-up fight-or-flight response. When he was a kid, he couldn't run from the neglect and loneliness. He had to just deal with it, so all that trauma was stored in his legs. And he points out this isn't "some mystical BS"—there are studies and data to back this up.

The weird thing is, besides that thought, nothing from his childhood came up. He felt like all the other therapy had helped him work through his childhood issues. What came up was everything he'd dealt with since his books became popular. For the last fifteen years, he'd taken tons of flak. He admits he deserved some of it, but he still took it. And he took it alone. He always assumed he was strong enough to just handle it. Turns out it did bother him, and he didn't even know it.

And that's what MDMA does—it tricks your brain into feeling safe so it can start to process hidden trauma. It lets the defensive walls down, and then you can see things your brain normally hides from you. In other words, the unconscious becomes conscious. The ego is quieted, and you can be honest with yourself.

Not everyone has to take MDMA to get to this place, but this is a place all of us should work toward. For Tucker, it changed everything. His anger levels dropped dramatically. A few weeks after taking MDMA, he was shocked when Southwest messed up his ticket and he didn't lose his shit. "A month before…I would have screamed at people," he said. He was annoyed, but it didn't lead to anger. He found that "astounding."[4]

He also got interesting feedback from his team after meetings. They said things like, "You seem lighter," and, "Your intensity was there, but it seemed happy and fun, less stress and pressure." They said he went out of his way "to be generous and compliment people" and that "the underlying sense of discontentment" was gone.[5]

Tucker wasn't trying to act differently—he *was* different. But one thing he noticed was that he was afraid to let go of his anger. It served a purpose for him—it was how he got things done. He said, "Anger chases away fear. It makes me feel powerful…I use it as fuel to succeed."[6]

He thinks that's why some of us don't want to let go of our problems: We find a way to use them to our advantage. They're negative, yes, but they have a positive benefit too. "And *that*," he wrote, "is the most fearful thing, and *that* is why most people are so resistant to deep change, and to letting go of things."[7]

After a few sessions of MDMA, he said he felt "calmer, so much more settled and at home in myself. I can't even believe how I used to be on a day-to-day basis."[8]

Ultimately, Tucker realized he'd been held back by not dealing with his anger and by not facing the stress he'd been under for the last fifteen years.

An Unexpected Transformation

This led to him, as he described it, "playing small and afraid." He had a power and ability in him he wasn't using "because I let all of that shit pile up, unprocessed, and it choked my life force."[9]

Tucker said he realized he needed to go from being a "warrior" to being a "builder." Warriors fight alone. And Tucker did that for years—as a kid, in college, then as an author building his persona and fighting his critics. But now, it was time for him to build, and that required "a very different type of courage. And a different mindset." He needed "patience, vision, and persuasion," and most importantly, "a lot of people…No one builds alone."[10]

You'll Do the Work Either Way

So, why am I diving so deep into Tucker's story? Because, in a way, it's the story of you and me and everyone on Earth. We've all dealt with tough shit. We've all got baggage we don't know how to deal with or don't even know exists. And it's holding us back from our true potential.

Here's what Tucker wrote about this:

"Your brain is ALWAYS processing the trauma.

You CANNOT AVOID processing the trauma. There is no other way past it.

The ONLY question is, do you process it consciously or unconsciously?

You WILL do the work either way.

If you do it unconsciously, you'll probably do things that are destructive to your life. Addiction, anger, self-abuse, overachievement, etc."[11]

Tucker's come a long way, and it's because he chose to process the trauma consciously. He asked for help. He admitted he needed to change. Then he put in the work. And the process isn't done—he's still digging and trying new ways to be better.

He's married now—has been for almost ten years. He has four kids and lives on a ranch in Texas. He gave up his party lifestyle a long time ago. He still writes, still has an edge and tells the uncensored truth, but it all comes from a better place now.

So, can a leader change? Well, if Tucker Max can do it, I think just about anyone can.

If you're wondering if there's hope for you, I guarantee there is.

We Don't Want to See Our Leaders Fail

Lots of people out there believe there's hope for you too. If you remember all the way back to chapter 1 and my leadership survey, I asked people, "Do you think a bad leader can change?" Almost half—47%—said yes.

Now, you could look at that number and think it's low. But it basically means that one out of two members of your team believes in your ability to be a better leader.

So, what about the other half? Well, they'll believe it when they see it. And that's fine. Most of your team wants a better relationship with you. According to psychologist Michelle McQuaid's research, 70% of workers said they'd be happier if they got along better with their boss. And that goes up to 80% for workers in their 20s and 30s. So, those millennials and Gen Zers are especially ready for you to be the leader that they're happy to see.[12]

If you haven't been the best leader in the past, that's okay. There's no time like the present to start becoming the leader you were meant to be.

Chapter 14

How Do Leaders Change?

A few years ago, I attended a conference of business owners and leaders. During one of the sessions the speaker pulled out a No. 2 pencil and asked us what we thought about it.

Most of us talked about how it reminded us of our early days at school. You remember taking tests with a No. 2 pencil? Well, maybe you don't. With smartphones and laptops, you don't see many people using pencils these days.

The presenter went on to talk about how one day his mentor gave him a pencil with an eraser to remind him of five important lessons an eraser can teach us.

- **Lesson 1:** Erasers allow us to correct mistakes, and mistakes *are* correctable. Everyone makes them. You have to erase them and let go.
- **Lesson 2:** Erasers give us the power to adjust, and our best work requires adjustments and updates. Your goals and hopes and dreams absolutely must be written down, but they need to be written in pencil. The world and your situation will change. The eraser will help you be more flexible and adaptable.
- **Lesson 3:** Erasers give us a safety net and remind us that the pressure isn't as great as we might think. If you write in pen, there is pressure to get the answers right the first time. Having an eraser takes off some of that pressure.

How Do Leaders Change?

- **Lesson 4:** Erasers invite us to edit. Results of a second (or third) draft are almost always better. If you don't succeed the first time, the eraser lets you make edits and try again.
- **Lesson 5:** Erasers erase the past in our minds and help us focus on what's next. Yes, you must learn from the past, but after processing it in a healthy way, you let it go and stay forward-focused.

If anyone could have lingered on their mistakes, it was Tucker Max. He sold millions of books filled with stories about the awful things he did—talk about oversharing. But he found a healthier path forward. He knew that all he could do is be the best version of himself *now*.

Remember Lee Cockerell? His leadership style put a man in the hospital. It put Lee in the hospital too—more than once!—when members of his team attacked him. Yet he changed and kept moving forward. By the end of his career, he was leading forty thousand people across twenty Disney resorts and four theme parks. And he created the leadership training program at Disney that developed seven thousand leaders. He didn't let his past mistakes define him or determine his future. Today, he speaks all over the world, inspiring leaders to bring magic into their organizations.

I realize you can't actually erase the past. But you can imagine that you've got a clean slate. You can choose not to dwell on the mistakes you've made and not be bogged down by guilt or shame.

Let's do a quick exercise. Take a moment to think about a mistake you've made in the last week. It could be a leadership mistake or a mistake with your family or friends. Now, imagine that moment was written in pencil. If you could pull out your eraser and rewrite it, what would you do differently?

Next time you're in a similar situation, you've got a new script—a new and better way to act that reflects who you want to be.

That's the power of using your eraser. It helps you learn from failure.

As you begin transforming your leadership brand, let go of the guilt and shame of past failures—but hold on to the lessons you learned from them. There's no escaping past mistakes entirely. But you're not doomed to repeat them. And they don't have to weigh you down. Erasing and rewriting lets you see how to be better next time and frees you so you're not defined by the things you've done.

Create Space for Curiosity

When I look at guys like Lee Cockerell and Tucker Max, I think, *Why did they change?* These were two extreme assholes. If you met them in their asshole prime, you'd think there was no hope for them. What was the catalyst that made them take a different path? Do they have something in common?

I think they do: curiosity. That might seem like an odd answer, but hear me out. Both of these guys have always been learners, ready and willing to take in new information. If there was a way to get better, they sought it out. In other words, they're curious. At some point in both of their lives, that curiosity turned on themselves—*Why do I do the things I do? Why am I acting this way?*

Once they started asking those questions, what'd they do next? They got feedback. They went about it in different ways, probably based on the different generations they're part of, but it amounted to the same thing. Tucker went on a years-long quest to figure himself out through therapy. Lee took a different approach, and I want to dig into that a little now. We've tackled Tucker's bio, but we haven't talked much about Lee's. The interesting thing is, they've got a similar arc.

Lee was born into poverty and grew up on a farm with no indoor plumbing. He never met his father. His mother was married five times. And he was adopted twice. He's actually on his third name. He started out as Norwood Deal, then it was Lee Lemmons, then he became Lee Cockerell at age sixteen when he was adopted again.

Lee called his childhood "dysfunctional." As you can imagine, it left some scars. But being a baby boomer, Lee didn't really dwell on it much.

How Do Leaders Change?

He went off to college and flunked out. He said he had too much fun and didn't study (sounds like Tucker). He tried the Army next and excelled. When he left the Army and started his professional career, employers loved him. "I got things done, man," he told me. "I'm organized. When I give you something that I need by five o'clock Friday, God help you. I abused the authority."

This was the '60s. Most leaders had come out of World War II, and no one was interested in your opinions. You followed orders. Lee said, "I thought that's the way it's supposed to be. Over time, I was so effective and disciplined that I kept getting promoted." He said his bosses didn't care about his bad behavior because they loved the results he got.

I already told you about Lee's wake-up call when a hotel manager had a panic attack over Lee's visit. This was in the '80s—twenty years into Lee's career. It took him that long to start to rethink who he was. And that wasn't entirely Lee's fault. At work, he said, "Everybody was telling me I was doing a great job…I was getting promoted, getting the stock options, the cars, all the stuff." But a part of him knew he shouldn't be treating people this way.

So, how did he move forward? The first thing he did was talk to his wife. She asked him a question that set him on a new path: "Do you really want to be *that* guy?" Lee didn't.

Lee said, "I started going to some leadership classes and seminars. Listening. Reading more. Trying to understand more." In other words, Lee got curious, and he went looking for answers.

This process probably felt a little risky. Just like Tucker said, sometimes our dysfunctions serve a purpose for us. We learn to use them to our advantage. Lee was at the height of his career, and whatever he was doing, it was working. Would he fail if he changed his leadership style?

Lee pressed forward anyway. He knew that what got him here was not going to get him there. Being an asshole was not the right path for him.

And he was right. After that, his career soared. And more importantly, he could be proud of the way he led.

The Leader Who Won't Change

So what happens when a leader doesn't change? Obviously, there's not one simple answer to that question, but I think Travis Kalanick is a good example of what can go wrong when a leader doesn't evolve.

If you don't know Travis, he's the former CEO of Uber. I highly recommend the TV series *Super Pumped: The Battle for Uber*. It's an entertaining and true story about Travis' rise and fall.

In the early days of Uber, Travis was exactly what the company needed. He was the classic "warrior"—incredibly competitive and ready for a fight. And Uber had plenty of fights. They were battling a taxi industry that'd spent a lot of money lobbying local governments to pass laws that benefited them. They weren't about to give up their monopoly to some start-up company.

So Travis was often up against city hall—about the toughest opponent you can have. Without going into detail, I'll just say he found "creative" ways to grow his company.

And it worked. Uber battled their way to the top. But 2017 was the year it all came crashing down—for Travis at least. He'd become a liability to the company and its investors. Allegations started flooding in that year: toxic work environment, sexism, sexual harassment, ethics violations, shady practices, visiting brothels on the company dime. Then three things happened that really sent things spiraling. He joined Trump's economic advisory team, which was an unpopular move among his mostly urban customers. He seemed to side against the striking New York City taxi drivers, which made him look anti-immigrant and anti-driver. Then a video was leaked of him arguing with an Uber driver about new pricing policies.

After that, a #deleteUber campaign launched on Twitter and thousands of people were deleting the app every day.

Uber's investors went after Travis hard. They needed him to step aside or the company would keep losing money. A public apology wasn't going to cut it. Travis was forced out as CEO in the middle of 2017.

How Do Leaders Change?

What got Travis here was not going to get him there. He needed to shift from warrior to builder, but he just didn't seem to understand that, or maybe he wasn't capable of changing. Right up until the end, he considered fighting the investors and the board, but his mentor Arianna Huffington talked him into resigning. He just had one condition: He wanted Bill Gurley, the board member and investor who spearheaded his resignation, to leave too. He told Arianna: "One champion to another, if I'm not wearing the belt, neither is he."[1]

In the last scene in *Super Pumped*, Travis sees Bill and lets him know he's responsible for getting him kicked off the board. Bill acts like it doesn't matter to him, and Travis doesn't buy it. He tells Bill, "For warriors, the field of battle is all that ever matters."[2]

For Travis, nothing mattered but the win. The problem was, he focused on battles instead of the war. He should've stopped asking, *How do I win?* and started asking, *What would a great leader do in this situation?* He couldn't get out of his own way and play the long game.

You might be thinking, *He's a billionaire—he won!* Well, this isn't a book about making money. This is a book about being a great leader. And in the end, Travis had no one to lead. His entire team turned on him—they lost faith in him. They saw that the road he was on was a dead end.

The Curiosity Muscle

In *The Curiosity Muscle*, authors Diana Kander and Andy Fromm talk about the "plateau effect," which is when companies experience a period of amazing success but then can't grow afterwards. To become successful, they usually innovated in wildly creative ways. But as those same innovations lose their power, the company keeps trying to use them. They fail because they try to repeat past successes rather than forging new paths.

It's not a big jump to apply the plateau effect to individuals. Looking at Travis Kalanick, he couldn't make the transition from bad-boy CEO of a disruptive start-up to billion-dollar leader of a multinational corporation.

226

So, what could Travis have done differently? I think some insights from *The Curiosity Muscle* could have helped him. First, as the title says, curiosity is a muscle. You've got to use it or lose it. And you've got to be curious enough to be wrong. You've got to be okay with the fact that if you go poking around trying to figure out how to be better, you might find out that you're the problem.

Second, you have to regularly ask yourself two questions:

1. What are my blind spots?
2. How can I get help to solve these blind spots?

We talked about blind spots in chapter 2. They're weak spots in your life that you just can't see. If you can't see them, how can you know they exist? By getting feedback. That's why I'm such a big proponent of doing a Leadership Brand 360 Survey (see chapter 2). And it's not a one-and-done thing. You need to do a 360 once a year, at least.

Getting feedback is tough. You're asking people in your life to call out your shit. But if you don't do that, you'll never know what it is, which means you'll never be able to fix it.

Once you get feedback, take it seriously. Then ask yourself, *How can I get help to solve this?*

You see this progression in Tucker Max and Lee Cockerell. They had a sense they were messed up in some way, they got feedback from people (solicited and unsolicited) about their blind spots, then they went searching for ways to fix themselves.

Listen, we're under a lot of pressure as leaders—from our organizations, our leaders, our teams, our families, and our investors. It's not easy. But our people want to see us succeed, and they're willing to give us a chance.

Tucker Max changed. Lee Cockerell changed. So can you.

How Do Leaders Change?

Don't fall into the trap that Travis Kalanick fell into. Here's how to avoid it:

1. Understand the five pressure points from chapter 11.
2. Stay curious.
3. Welcome feedback from your team and your family. And if you need to, get help from a counselor or other professional.
4. Really hear what they're saying.
5. Use their feedback to get better and make positive changes.

Now it's time to move on to the last section of the book: Developing Your Leadership Brand. It's time to put what you've learned into action in your everyday life.

Part V

Developing Your Leadership Brand

Chapter 15

Putting in the Work

I've shared my journey, my struggles, and the steps I took to become the leader people are happy to see. Throughout this book, I've spoken about the challenges I faced, the decisions I made, and the lessons I learned along the way. But now the focus shifts—it's your turn.

The challenge before you is to take everything you've absorbed—the insights, the lessons, and the strategies—and put them into action. It's time for you to roll up your sleeves and become the kind of leader who inspires, empowers, and truly makes a difference in the lives of those you lead.

The last challenge in your journey to becoming the leader people are happy to see is overcoming Resistance (yes, with a capital R). Earlier in the book, we explored how ego can often get in the way, blinding us to our flaws and making it harder to lead with humility. We also discussed the five pressure points that every leader must confront. But Resistance is different—it's a force that quietly works against you, trying to keep you stuck, comfortable, and complacent. It shows up as doubt, procrastination, or fear, convincing you that change is too hard or unnecessary. But if you want to truly lead, you must face Resistance head on. This is your final test—the point where you either push through or stay where you are. Now is the time to commit to the work, silence the Resistance, and step fully into the role of a leader people are genuinely happy to follow.

Best-selling author Steven Pressfield explores the concept of Resistance in his book *The War of Art*. He describes it as that invisible, destructive force that rises up against any act of creation, progress, or self-improvement. It's the voice that tells you, "Maybe tomorrow," or, "You're not ready yet." It's the subtle doubt, procrastination, or fear that keeps you from taking action. This is the Resistance you'll face as you try to become the leader you want to be—the leader your team deserves. Your ego and the pressure points were just the beginning; now you must confront this unseen enemy that tries to stop you from moving forward. The battle against Resistance is the final step. The question is: Will you push through it or let it stop you?

What separates the reluctant leader from the professional leader is commitment—and the key to that commitment is intentionality. The reluctant leader hesitates, waiting for the right moment, letting fear and self-doubt dictate their actions. They're guided by excuses, easily sidetracked by distractions, and often avoid the uncomfortable truths that come with real growth. In contrast, the professional leader operates with purpose and intentionality, showing up consistently and making deliberate choices to grow and lead, even when it's hard. The professional leader knows that leadership isn't about being perfect. It's about taking ownership, learning from mistakes, and pushing through challenges.

I remember when my business partner Steve and I attended the EntreLeadership Summit together. That was a turning point for us. We walked out of that summit with a new sense of clarity and determination. We made a conscious decision to stop acting like amateurs and start leading with intention. We recognized that being passive or casual in our approach was holding us back, and that's when we fully committed to becoming professional leaders. From that moment on, we approached leadership as a craft to be mastered, not just a role to fill. It was the shift from being reactive to being intentional that transformed us from amateur leaders into professional ones.

Can you imagine a professional athlete saying they're not going to practice or put in the effort every day to get better? Of course not. In the world of sports, professionals know that consistent effort, discipline, and intentional practice are the foundation of their success. They don't skip workouts or avoid the drills that challenge them because they understand that every day they don't push themselves, someone else is getting ahead. The same is true in leadership. You can't lead effectively without putting in the work. Just like a pro athlete, a professional leader shows up, commits to constant improvement, and treats every day as an opportunity to sharpen their skills and elevate their team. Anything less is the mindset of an amateur.

It's now time to do the work. You've gained the tools, insights, and strategies to become the leader people are happy to see, but none of it matters if you don't take action. Leadership isn't a title or a destination—it's a daily practice. Just like the professional athlete who trains every day, you need to commit to showing up, being intentional, and putting in the effort to grow. The journey ahead won't always be easy, and Resistance will try to stop you, but this is where you dig in. This is where you go from knowing what needs to be done to actually doing it. It's time to take the lessons, apply them, and become the leader you're meant to be.

The Story of Sarah

I once had a leader who worked for me—let's call her Sarah—who had just been promoted to a management position. Sarah had been successful throughout her entire career. People loved her, and she had always been able to achieve great results by relying on her natural abilities and strong work ethic. However, as she transitioned into this new leadership role, she quickly realized that what had gotten her here wasn't going to get her to the next level. Leading at this stage required something different—skills and approaches she hadn't yet developed.

In the beginning, Sarah leaned heavily on her title, expecting her team to follow her because she was "the boss." She assumed that her past success and position would naturally translate into respect and trust from her team. But as time went on, it became clear that her team wasn't inspired. Their engagement was low, and they seemed to follow her instructions out of obligation rather than genuine enthusiasm.

During one particularly challenging time, Sarah confided in me that she felt like she was trapped in what she described as "tactic hell"—constantly reacting to problems, putting out fires, and feeling like she was in a state of chaos. This was when we had a critical conversation about what it means to "turn pro" as a leader.

I explained to Sarah that "turning pro" means making a commitment to leadership as a craft—not as a position, but as a daily practice that requires discipline, growth, and intentionality. Professionals don't rely on natural talent or their title alone; they show up every day, ready to put in the work, improve their skills, and make thoughtful decisions. A pro leader understands that leadership is about consistency, resilience, and personal responsibility. It's about pushing through resistance, whether that resistance comes from within or from external challenges. In essence, turning pro means leaving behind the amateur mindset that says leadership is something you achieve, and adopting the mindset that leadership is something you *practice*.

Sarah took that lesson to heart. One of the first steps she took was to sit down and write out her leadership brand. She took the time to identify and understand the five pressure points that were affecting her mindset and performance as a leader. At times, she felt overwhelmed, almost as if she were constantly fighting to stay afloat. But Sarah realized something crucial: No one was going to bail her out, and no one was coming to save her. She had to take full responsibility for making things better—not just for herself, but for her team.

From that point on, Sarah began shifting her focus. She invested time in developing her team, learning about their individual strengths and weaknesses, and providing them with opportunities to grow. At the same time, she committed to her own growth as a leader—reading leadership books, attending workshops, and practicing active listening. She embraced the idea that leadership is a craft that requires daily work, just like how a professional athlete trains or an artist hones their skills.

Over time, her team began to see the difference. They started to follow her not because they had to, but because they genuinely wanted to. Sarah had "turned pro," and that shift in mindset made all the difference—not only for her own leadership development, but also for the success and trust within her team.

How to Put Your Leadership Brand into Action

So, how do you start doing the work? What does it look like to put your leadership brand into action?

Let's do a few quick exercises to figure this out. First, I want you to think about what you're good at as a leader. Write down five things you do well.

As a Leader, What Am I Good At?

1. _____
2. _____
3. _____
4. _____
5. _____

Now think about areas you'd like to change. What do you struggle with? These could be things like getting angry, micromanaging, motivating your team, etc.

Putting in the Work

As a Leader, What Do I Struggle With?

1. _____
2. _____
3. _____
4. _____
5. _____

Okay, now think about what new skills you'd like to develop as a leader. These could be things like being a better communicator or negotiator or learning better time-management techniques.

What New Skills Would I Like to Develop as a Leader?

1. _____
2. _____
3. _____
4. _____
5. _____

Lastly, think about what might be causing you to fail as a leader. This one's hard because it forces you to look in the mirror and ask, *Am I the problem?* But I want you to think about this from an external standpoint too—not just an internal one. Think back to those five pressure points from chapter 11 (your organization, leaders, team, family, investors/board). Which pressure points are you concerned with right now?

What Might Be Causing Me to Fail as a Leader?
(Remember to include internal *and* external causes.)

1. _____
2. _____
3. _____
4. _____
5. _____

Now let's take a look at your lists and make action steps for each one. For your first list—what you're good at—there's just one action step: Keep doing what you're doing. For the rest, we'll go more in depth.

What You're Struggling With

Let's start with what you're struggling with. Take a look at the table below. Write down the five things you're struggling with, then write what you're going to do to change them over the next ninety days.

What I'm Struggling With	What I'll Do to Change It Over the Next 90 Days
1.	
2.	
3.	
4.	
5.	

Putting in the Work

Every week, evaluate how you're doing with each item. I'd suggest creating a spreadsheet or even just a handwritten table (see next page for example) so you can track your progress and make notes about where you failed, what you got right, and how to improve.

You'll have good weeks and bad weeks. That's okay. The point is to keep what you're struggling with front and center—that's what will allow you to make progress.

Ask your team how you're doing. Feedback is critical. If you do this right and keep track of your weekly progress, your team and your leaders will notice the difference.

Let me give you an example of what this looks like. When I was in Ramsey's EntreLeadership program, I'd do weekly video calls with a group of other leaders. There was a guy named Chris in the group, and he'd always stay quiet the whole call. He'd just take everything in, then toward the end, he'd finally speak up and say something. And whatever he said was so insightful. You know why? Because he listened.

I took this to heart. Whenever I was in a meeting at work, I'd always think, "Be like Chris. Be like Chris." And this was hard for me! I like to talk, I like to share what's on my mind. But I wanted to listen more and talk less. Once I started being like Chris, my team took notice. I got feedback from them that mentioned how much they loved that I asked more questions in meetings and how I took a back seat and let them talk more. That's the kind of feedback you're looking for as you work on what you're struggling with.

Example of Table for the Next 90 Days (13 Weeks)

I'm Struggling With:	What I'll Do to Change It	Week 1 Notes and Feedback	Week 2 Notes and Feedback	Week 3 Notes and Feedback
1 Micromanaging	I'll lay out a problem and empower my team to solve it. I won't interfere unless they come to me for help.	I felt like they were taking too long to come up with a solution, so I asked for an update. Oops. Should have trusted their process.	The solution they brought was fantastic. Now, I'm going to let them work on it and stick to the same hands-off approach.	I didn't like the SaaS platform they chose and tried to intervene. But I caught myself and let them move forward. My bias is just a personal preference—not a legitimate issue.
2. Getting angry				
3. Motivating my team				
4.				
5.				

What New Skills Would You Like to Develop

For this list, you'll just pick one skill that you'd like to learn and then work on that for ninety days. For instance, if you want to learn negotiation, that's your focus for the next ninety days. Read books on negotiation, take courses, go to conferences, watch YouTube videos—whatever it takes.

Pick the first skill you want to learn and write it below. Then write a plan to master this skill over the next ninety days. Once the ninety days are up, you can move on to the next skill. It's probably a good idea to do some research before you make your plan. Find out what books you should read, who the gurus for this skill are, what courses you could take, what conferences you could go to, and what podcasts to listen to. Create a checklist here for your overall plan, but make sure to create a weekly checklist, too, so you stay on top of learning your new skill.

Skill I'd Like to Learn	My 90-Day Plan to Master It
	○
	○
	○
	○
	○

What Might Be Causing You to Fail

Lastly, we've got the list for what might be causing you to fail. The first thing you can do is recognize these forces. Understand them for what they are and how they are affecting you.

Second, write down the reason why that thing is stopping you from being the leader you want to be. Take a minute to do that now for each list item.

Next, is there something you can do about it, or is it just what it is? If there is something you can do about it, then write a plan for how you'll make changes. If not, then how are you going to work with it? Sometimes change isn't possible.

For instance, my leadership brand clashed big time with the company that acquired Advoco. So, the force working against me was the organization. Could I change it? Nope. This company was a machine. Could I successfully work with it? Also, nope. So, I left.

My friend Javier also worked at a company that clashed with his leadership brand, but he found ways to make it work. He made his little corner of the company a haven where he led his team well. That's worked for him for decades.

Every situation is different. Evaluate yours and fill out the table below.

What's Causing Me to Fail	Why Is It Stopping Me from Being the Leader I Want to Be?	Can I Change It? (Yes/No)	If Yes, What's My Plan to Fix It?
1.			
2.			
3.			
4.			
5.			

Lastly, let's do one final exercise before we close this section of the book. Let's go back to your leadership brand—to the list of those five words you'd like to hear people say about you. Take a look at your original list from chapter 2. Is there anything you would change? Go ahead and make any adjustments now and write your final list below.

Putting in the Work

My Leadership Brand

1. _____

2. _____

3. _____

4. _____

5. _____

There it is—that's what you're aiming for. That's who you're going to become. Put this list on your car's dashboard or on your bathroom mirror. You want to see it constantly. It will help you remember what you're shooting for every day, in every interaction, and in every moment.

And one last thing: Get feedback from your team on a regular basis. It's vitally important, and I can't stress it enough. Send out Leadership Brand 360 Surveys. That's how you'll know if you're making progress and becoming a better leader.

Well, we've come to the end of the road. I want to thank you for getting this far, and I sincerely hope this book has made a difference in your life and leadership.

A famous quote says that champions are made when no one is watching. Well, leaders are made when everyone is watching. It's tough to be out front—the pressure is real. But it's a rewarding path, especially when you can look back and be proud of how you led.

I've included a few more thoughts in the Conclusion. It's a brief section meant to remind you why all this leadership brand stuff really matters.

Now, go become the leader people are happy to see. I wish you the best.

Conclusion

The Legacy of Leadership

Last year, my father-in-law, Curtis Bagwell, passed away at the age of eighty-five. As our family prepared for his funeral, the minister asked us to share any reflections on Curtis's life. It struck me how we often wait until the end to express how we truly feel about someone, but I suppose that's just how it goes.

For me, writing about Curtis was simple. He was someone who lived his life serving others, and as I sat down to write, the words flowed naturally. Curtis lived like he wanted to be remembered, and it made me realize something profound: *If you want to live a great life, then live like you want to be remembered.*

Curtis truly embodied this idea. Above all else, he loved his family—his wife and three children. He found joy in providing for them and making them feel special. But Curtis's sense of family extended beyond his household. He cared deeply for his work family, too, and he loved to work. Yes, he was a bit of a workaholic, but not for selfish reasons. Curtis worked to enrich the lives of those around him—his coworkers, employees, and clients. Business was personal for Curtis, and he treated everyone as if they were family. I heard time and again from people who knew him how much they loved and appreciated him for making them feel special.

One of his longtime colleagues, a dentist, visited Curtis while he was recovering from a hospital stay. The dentist didn't just talk about how Curtis helped him professionally—he spoke of what a great and beloved friend Curtis was. Curtis had an incredible ability to make people feel valued.

We get one chance in life to do it right, and Curtis got it right. Every day, I'm grateful that I got to call him my father-in-law. I'm thankful for the lessons he taught me about being a man, a husband, a father, and a businessman. I'm thankful for the stories of love and respect that his colleagues and clients shared about him. Curtis lived a life full of love, and in return, love surrounded him.

I Dare You

I share these thoughts with you to ask: *How do you want to be remembered?* Developing an amazing leadership brand is about more than professional success. The money, titles, and status won't matter in the end. What matters is how you make people feel—that's what people will remember.

While sorting through some of my grandfather's things, I found an old book titled *I Dare You*. Inside, there was an inscription from a friend that read, "Life is a challenge. Are you willing to accept it? I dare you." This was written back in 1952, but the sentiment rings true today. Life has always been a challenge, regardless of the time or generation. The real question is, are we willing to accept the challenge to become the person we're meant to be?

So, I've got a dare for you. *I dare you not to be a jerk. I dare you to lead not by fear or anger, but with grace and a servant's heart.* I dare you to dig deep within yourself and find that warrior with a kind heart. I dare you to dream big and understand that life is a journey—not one event or moment defines you.

Now, go and become the leader you were meant to be. I dare you.

Chapter 33

In Memory of Chris Oakley

In Chapter 7, I shared the story of my business coach and dear friend, Chris Oakley, and how he taught me one of the most important lessons of my life. At just twenty-eight years old, Chris wrote his own obituary. He was so young, but already thinking deeply about his legacy and what he wanted to be remembered for. That simple yet profound act shaped his path forward. It gave him clarity on life and leadership, and it inspired me to think about my own path in a way I never had before.

Tragically, on December 12, 2019, Chris passed away in a hunting accident at the age of thirty-seven. If you noticed that I numbered this chapter 33, it's because Chris had a special connection to that number. It was the number he wore on all his basketball jerseys, inspired by his favorite player, Larry Bird. This chapter is dedicated to Chris, in honor of his impact on my life and the lives of many others.

My journey with Chris began when he became my business coach through the EntreLeadership program. But he quickly became more than just a coach—he became a mentor and a dear friend. We spoke every week, and I would often visit him in Nashville. Chris had an incredible gift for making people feel special, like they truly mattered. At his funeral, one of the speakers asked the attendees to raise their hand if they considered Chris their best friend. To my amazement, every hand in the room went up. That says everything about the kind of person Chris was.

When Chris left the EntreLeadership team, I knew I had to find a way to keep him in my life. I hired him as my personal business coach and brought him in to coach my leadership team as well. Chris transformed us. He didn't see business as just business—it was personal. He believed that business, like life, was about building meaningful connections and helping others succeed.

When Chris visited our team in Greenville, he would spend time at my home with my family. He got to know all of us, and wow, could he make us laugh. He believed in me, and he had a way of simplifying the things that seemed complicated. He'd challenge me to be better in everything I did, always pushing me forward.

As I reflect on the lessons I learned from Chris, I'm reminded of the profound impact he had on my life and the lives of so many others. Chris believed deeply that life is a series of meaningful connections, and that each person we meet along the way shapes our journey in ways we may never fully understand. His mantra was always "doing less, better," a philosophy that true success comes not from doing more, but from focusing on what truly matters and doing it with excellence.

Chris understood something fundamental that I have written about in this book—*the importance of leadership brand*. He knew that his legacy, or "brand," would not be defined by his professional accomplishments alone, but by how he made people feel and the impact he had on their lives. Chris embodied the idea that leadership is about serving others and building authentic, lasting relationships. He was intentional about the decisions he made and the people he surrounded himself with, because he knew that those things shaped not only his personal brand, but the direction of his life and his leadership.

Recently, I reread Chris's obituary. He had written it when he was twenty-eight, and as I read it, I realized how much of it had come true. In his obituary, he wrote about founding a coaching company to "help Christian business owners win in the marketplace and leverage their influence for Kingdom impact." A few years later, he made that vision a reality.

I'll never forget what Chris told me when I hesitated to write my own obituary. I've always been uncomfortable with the thought of death, but Chris didn't let that fear stop me. He said, "If you don't face your own mortality, how will you know if you're on the right path? You need to live your life the way you want to be remembered." In that moment, everything became clear.

Life is fleeting, and it's easy to believe that the present moment will last forever. We take our loved ones, our friends, our teams, even our everyday lives for granted. But without a clear purpose, without a defined goal, we lose sight of what truly matters.

Chris often reminded me of the Latin phrase *memento mori*—"remember you will die." While it may seem like a somber thought, it's not about focusing on death. It's about focusing on life and living fully. It's about appreciating the present moment and recognizing the beauty around us.

As Chris often said, focus on:
- What's important to you
- Protecting your time—your most valuable resource
- Noticing and appreciating the beauty in each moment
- Being honest, because you may not have time for forgiveness later

It's time we start living like we want to be remembered.

Looking back on my time with Chris, I am struck by his wisdom, his kindness, and his commitment to living out his values. He was more than a gifted business coach—he was a true friend and mentor. He touched countless lives with his generosity and his deep belief in the power of human connection. Chris's leadership brand was unmistakable, and it wasn't about titles or accolades. It was about the way he made people feel—valued, inspired, and important. That is the essence of leadership.

I know Chris would be proud of the lessons shared in this book, and my hope is that you will take them to heart. Live an inspired life. Strive to be better in everything you do. And most importantly, think about how you want to be remembered—*because your leadership brand is being shaped every single day.*

Lastly, don't wait to tell the people around you how much they mean to you. Let them know they're important and loved. Take time out of your busy schedule to reach out and connect with those who matter. By doing so, we strengthen our relationships and become the people we are meant to be.

I'm Marty, and I hope you make every minute count.

Sources

Introduction

1 Simon Sinek, *Start With Why*, Portfolio, 2009.//
2 David Ogilvy, *Ogilvy on Advertising*, Random House, 1985.

Chapter 1

1 Department of Leadership and Law, U.S. Naval Academy, *Fundamentals of Naval Leadership,* Naval Institute Press, 1984.

2 Stephen Covey, "The Leader Formula: The 4 Things That Make a Good Leader," www.stephencovey.com. https://web.archive.org/web/20110723000458/http://www.stephencovey.com/blog/?p=6. Published December 10, 2007. Accessed March 5, 2024.

3 Simon Sinek, *The Infinite Game*. Portfolio, 2019.

4 Jill Avery and Rachel Greenwald, "A new approach to building your personal brand," *Harvard Business Review*, May-June, 2023, https://hbr.org/2023/05/a-new-approach-to-building-your-personal-brand.

5 *The Matrix*, directed and written by the Wachowskis, Burbank, CA: Warner Brothers, 1999.

6 Jerzy Gregorek, guest, The Tim Ferris Show, #228 "The Lion of Olympic Weightlifting, 62-Year-Old Jerzy Gregorek," March 16, 2017, https://tim.blog/2017/03/16/jerzy-gregorek/.

7 Andy Stanley, *The Principle of the Path*. Thomas Nelson, 2011.

8 Bo Burlingham, *Small Giants: Companies That Chose to Be Great Instead of Big*, Portfolio, 2016.

Chapter 2

1 Arianna Huffington, *Thrive: The Third Metric to Redefining Success and Creating a Life of Well-Being, Wisdom, and Wonder*, Harmony Books, 2015.

2 Michelle McQuaid. *5 Reasons to Tell Your Boss to Go Fuck Themselves*, Michelle McQuaid, 2012.

3 McQuaid, *5 Reasons*.

4 McQuaid, *5 Reasons*.

5 Leonardo da Vincie, *The Notebooks of Leonardo da Vinci*, Prabhat Books, 2008.

6 John Maxwell, "Leadership Blind Spots," johnmaxwell.com, September 22, 2015, https://www.johnmaxwell.com/blog/leadership-blind-spots/.

7 John Maxwell, guest, Impact Theory with Tom Bilyeu, "If you're struggling to stay motivated, you need to watch this," February 4, 2020, YouTube, 19:20, https://www.youtube.com/watch?app=desktop&v=T9WIWz5PEQk

Chapter 3

1 *A Knight's Tale*, directed and written by Brian Helgeland, Culver City, CA: Sony Pictures Releasing, 2001.

2 Sean Covey, Jum Huling, Chris McChesney, *The 4 Disciplines of Execution: Achieving Your Wildly Important Goals*, Free Press, 2012, (emphasis mine).

3 "Meaningful Specific," Ziglar.com, accessed March 4, 2023, https://www.ziglar.com/quotes/meaningful-specific/.

4 Patrick Lencioni, *The Advantage: Why Organizational Health Trumps Everything Else in Business*, Joessey-Bass, 2012.

Chapter 4

1 Eckhart Tolle, *The Power of Now*, Namaste Publishing, 1999.

Chapter 5

1 Zig Ziglar, *Great Quotes from Zig Ziglar*, Gramercy Publishing, 2005.

2 *Ted Lasso*, "So Long, Farewell," season 3, episode 12, directed by Declan Lowney, written by Brendan Hunt, Joe Kelly, Jason Sudeikis; Doozer, Ruby Tuna's Inc., Warner Bros., Universal Television, 2023.

Chapter 6

1 Jim Collins, *Good to Great*, HarperCollins Publishers, 2001.

2 Jim Collins, *Good to Great*.

Chapter 7

1 Chip and Dan Heath, *The Power of Moments*, Simon & Schuster, 2017.

2 Chip and Dan Heath, *The Power of Moments*.

3 Andy Stanley, *The Principle of the Path*, Thomas Nelson, 2011.

Chapter 8

1 "Truman Quotes," Truman State University, accessed March 12, 2023, https://www.truman.edu/about/history/our-namesake/truman-quotes/.

2 Grace Mayer, "Charlie Munger's 'great lesson' of life: Cut out toxic people," *Business Insider*, November 28, 2023, https://www.businessinsider.com/billionaire-charlie-munger-business-advice-for-success-cut-toxic-people-2023-5.

3 *Moneyball*, directed by Bennett Miller, written by Aaron Sorkin and Steven Zaillian, Culver City, CA: Sony Pictures Releasing, 2011.

4 *Seinfeld*, "The Glasses," season 5, episode 3, directed by Tom Cherones, written by Tom Gammill and Max Pross, NBC, September 30, 1993.

5 Hal Elrod, *The Miracle Morning*, BenBella Books, Inc. , 2012.

6 Mel Robbins, *The 5 Second Rule*, Savio Republic, 2017.

7 Zig Ziglar, *See You at the Top*, Pelican Publishing Company, 2008.

8 Zig Ziglar, *See You at the Top*.

9 Zig Ziglar, "Zig Ziglar – Prime the Pump," uploaded by Attractualization, February 29, 2008, YouTube, https://www.youtube.com/watch?v=DdHAMjA1lMw.

Chapter 9

1 "Andy Stanley and Charles Stanley Speak at the Southern Baptist Pastors Conference," Hervict Jacobs Awaken Generation, October 19, 2011, https://awakengeneration.wordpress.com/2011/10/19/andy-stanley-and-charles-stanley-speak-at-the-southern-baptist-pastors-conference/.

2 Sean Covey, Jum Huling, Chris McChesney, *The 4 Disciplines of Execution: Achieving Your Wildly Important Goals*, Free Press, 2012, (emphasis mine).

3 Danny Meyer, *Setting the Table*, HarperCollins Publishers, 2006.

4 *Office Space*, directed and written by Mike Judge, Los Angeles: 20th Century Fox, 1999.

5 James Dyson, "The Dyson Story: James Dyson Speaks About Our Approach to Engineering," YouTube, uploaded by Dyson, March 6, 2020, https://www.youtube.com/watch?v=_hG79AwLw3s.

6 Steve Jobs, "Steve Jobs talks about managing people," YouTube, uploaded by ragni, June 12, 2010, https://www.youtube.com/watch?v=f60dheI4ARg.

7 Marcel Schwantes, "Warren Buffet Says You Can Ruin Your Life in 5 Minutes by Making 1 Critical Mistake," *Inc. Magazine*, November 6, 2021, https://www.inc.com/marcel-schwantes/warren-buffett-says-you-can-ruin-your-life-in-5-minutes-by-making-1-critical-mistake.html.

8 Stephen Covey, *The Speed of Trust*, Free Press, 2006.

Chapter 10

1 Simon Caulkin, "WL Gore: The Company Others Try and Fail to Imitate," *Financial Times*, August 1, 2019, https://www.ft.com/content/aee67fe0-ac63-11e9-b3e2-4fdf846f48f5.

2 Sara Blakely [@sarablakely] (May 30, 2024) "What is your 'why' for success? If you think money will solve your problems… it won't. I believe money magnifies," https://www.instagram.com/sarablakely/reel/C7nJq63MQEd/.

Chapter 11

1 Holy Bible, New International Version®, NIV® Copyright ©1973, 1978, 1984, 2011 by Biblica, Inc.® Used by permission. All rights reserved worldwide

Chapter 12

1 Natasha Lomas, "RIM's Lazaridis on why Qwerty's still working," *ZD Net*, May 16, 2008, https://www.zdnet.com/article/rims-lazaridis-on-why-qwertys-still-working/.

2 Richard Branson, guest, How I Built This with Guy Raz, "Virgin: Richard Branson," episode 21, January 30, 2017, https://www.npr.org/2017/01/30/511817806/virgin-richard-branson.

Chapter 13

1 Tucker Max, *I Hope They Serve Beer in Hell*, Citadel Publishing, 2009.

2 Tucker Max, "What MDMA Therapy Did for Me," tuckermax.com, August 28, 2019, https://www.tuckermax.com/what-mdma-therapy-did-for-me/.

3 Tucker Max, "What MDMA Therapy Did for Me"

4 Tucker Max, "What MDMA Therapy Did for Me"

5 Tucker Max, "What MDMA Therapy Did for Me"

6 Tucker Max, "What MDMA Therapy Did for Me"

7 Tucker Max, "What MDMA Therapy Did for Me"

8 Tucker Max, "What MDMA Therapy Did for Me"

9 Tucker Max, "What MDMA Therapy Did for Me"

10 Tucker Max, "What MDMA Therapy Did for Me"

11 Tucker Max, "What MDMA Therapy Did for Me"

12 Michelle McQuaid. *5 Reasons to Tell Your Boss to Go Fuck Themselves*, Michelle McQuaid, 2012.

Chapter 14

1 *Super Pumped: The Battle for Uber*, "Same Last Name," episode 7, directed by Zetna Fuentes, written by Brian Koppelman and David Levien, Showtime, April, 10, 2022.

Chapter 15

1 Steven Pressfield, *The War of Art*, Black Irish Entertainment, 2012.

2 Steven Pressfield, *The War of Art*

3 Steven Pressfield, *The War of Art*

4 Steven Pressfield, *The War of Art*

5 Steven Pressfield, *The War of Art*

6 Steven Pressfield, *The War of Art*

7 Steven Pressfield, *The War of Art*